FAVORITE
INDULGENCED PRAYERS

THE ADDED BENEFIT OF SAYING INDULGENCED PRAYERS

Saying prayers that have been indulgenced by the Church has the added benefit of enabling us to obtain the remission of the *temporal punishment* due for sins whose *guilt* has already been removed.

FAVORITE INDULGENCED PRAYERS

CONTAINING
SOME OF THE FINEST PRAYERS
FROM BOTH NEW AND OLD EDITIONS
OF THE *ENCHIRIDION OF INDULGENCES*

●

By
Anthony M. Buono

Illustrated

CATHOLIC BOOK PUBLISHING CORP.
New Jersey

NIHIL OBSTAT: Rev. Msgr. James M. Cafone, M.A., S.T.D.
Censor Librorum

IMPRIMATUR: ✠ Most Rev. John J. Myers, J.C.D., D.D.
Archbishop of Newark

(T-929)

2006 Catholic Book Publishing Corp., N.J.
Printed in the U.S.A

www.catholicbookpublishing.com

1 2 3 4 5 6 7 8 9 10

CONTENTS

FOREWORD

THE Church teaches that there are temporal punishments for sin. Even after receiving forgiveness for our sins, we must atone for them either in this life or in purgatory. We can do so in this life by deeds of penance comprising works or prayers.

Thus, we carry out the penance imposed in the Sacrament of Penance, which is usually the recitation of certain prayers. However, our sins are more serious than we think, and our penances are often slight.

Hence to help us in our frailty, the Church makes indulgences possible on our behalf. An indulgence is a remission of all or part of the temporal punishment due to sins that have already been forgiven.

From her spiritual treasury made up of Christ's merits (as well as those of Mary and the Saints), the Church grants the remission of the temporal punishment due to sin already forgiven—through indulgences attached to works and prayers.

Indulgenced works and prayers ultimately have as their purpose to bring us into closer union with Christ and the Church through charity. This should also be the basic reason for us to do the work or say the prayer graced with indulgences.

It is true that all prayers enable us to carry on a dialogue with God. However, indulgenced prayers have an added value because they have been time-tested by the Church and found to be very effective in helping people talk with God or the Saints. They also inculcate spiritual sentiments that work to lessen or do away with temporal punishment due to sin.

In other words, indulgenced prayers provide us with the mind of the Church, When praying such texts we can be sure that they reproduce sentiments that the Church wants the faithful to cultivate and possess.

The present book is intended to help Catholics make use of some of the best prayers from the official *Enchiridion of Indulgences.* By utilizing it, they can pray with the mind of the Church, with the words of our past brothers and sisters in Christ who make up the Communion of Saints, with the universal and timeless sentiments of the great masters of the spiritual life, and with some of the most beautiful writings of the inspired authors of Scripture.

At the same time, the prayers presented herein deal with important concerns of the Christian life. They can be used with full confidence that they will enhance the spiritual life of Catholics today.

Wherever possible, we have made use of the older translations of the indulgenced prayers, since these are the formulas most familiar to many of the faithful.

Every effort has been made to ensure that this book will be easy to use and attractive to the person praying. The text is printed in large pleasing typeface and in red and black. The inspiring colorful illustrations will help keep our minds on Jesus and through Him on the other Persons of the Blessed Trinity.

May all who use this prayerbook achieve a deeper and more vital spiritual life. May it lead them ever closer to the eternal union with the living God.

INDULGENCES—SPIRITUAL TREASURY OF THE CHURCH

From her spiritual treasury made up of Christ's merits (as well as those of Mary and the Saints), the Church grants the remission of the temporal punishment due to sin already forgiven—through indulgences attached to works and prayers.

FOUR GENERAL GRANTS
OF INDULGENCES

*F*ROM *the Council of Trent to the beginning of Vatican II, many Catholics had a particular fondness for prayers that were indulgenced by the Church. Undoubtedly, they felt that in reciting such prayers they were guarded from praying fruitlessly, so to speak. However, the precise nature of indulgences often escaped the faithful and abuses crept into the practice, so that they came to be used by some in an almost magical way.*

On January 1, 1967, Pope Paul VI promulgated new norms regarding the discipline of indulgences in the Church. The document dealt with the nature of sin, the punishment due to sin, the solidarity of all human beings in Adam and in Christ, the Communion of Saints, and the treasury of the expiations and merits of Christ, of the Blessed Virgin, and of the Saints—a treasury that has been given to the Church to be placed by her at the disposition of the faithful.

It also stressed how salutary is the use of indulgences, since they promote through charity the union of all the faithful with Christ and with the pastors of the Church, His representatives. At the same time it called for a revision of the indulgenced prayers and practices. This became a reality when a revised Latin edition of the Enchiridion of Indulgences *was published in 1968 and an English edition in 1969. (A later*

Latin edition appeared in 1986 that was substantially the same as the previous edition, and its 1991 English equivalent was entitled Handbook of Indulgences. *A millennium Latin edition appeared in 1999, but there is no official English edition yet. It too is substantially the same as the previous two.)*

The key idea of this new volume is the preeminent value of charity. The faithful are urged to look first of all to the worthy performance of their duties, with the assurance of obtaining not only greater merit but also a proportionate remission of temporal punishment for their sins already forgiven, this by virtue of both their personal effort and the gift of the Church.

This first major section presents the Introduction of the Enchiridion *as well as the new General Grants, so that the faithful can make use of them at opportune times and derive the greatest benefits from them.*

For the complete list of practices as well as a fuller treatment of indulgences, the reader is referred to the official English source for indulgences: the Enchiridion of Indulgences, *published in 1969 by Catholic Book Publishing Corp. or the latest edition, the* Handbook of Indulgences, *published in 1991 by the same firm.*

Introduction

1) An indulgence is the remission before God of the temporal punishment due for sins already forgiven as far as their guilt is concerned. This remission the faithful with the proper dispositions

and under certain determined conditions acquire through the intervention of the Church which, as minister of the Redemption, authoritatively dispenses and applies the treasury of the satisfaction won by Christ and the Saints.

2) An indulgence is partial or plenary, according as it removes either part or all of the temporal punishment due for sin.

3) No one, acquiring indulgences, can apply them to other living persons.

4) Partial as well as plenary indulgences can always be applied to the departed by way of suffrage.

5) The grant of a partial indulgence is designated only with the words "partial indulgence," without any determination of days or years.

6) The faithful, who at least with contrite heart perform an action to which a partial indulgence is attached, obtain, in addition to the remission of temporal punishment acquired by the action itself, an equal remission of punishment through the intervention of the Church,

7) The faithful, who devoutly use an *article of devotion* (crucifix or cross, rosary, scapular or medal) properly blessed by any priest, obtain a partial indulgence.

But if the *article of devotion* has been blessed by the Sovereign Pontiff or by any bishop, the faithful, using it devoutly, can also gain a plenary indulgence on the feast of the Holy Apostles, Peter and Paul, provided they also make a profession of faith according to any legitimate formula.

8) To be capable of gaining an indulgence for oneself, it is required that one be baptized, not excommunicated, in the state of grace at least at the completion of the prescribed works, and a subject of the one granting the indulgence.

9) In order that one who is capable may actually gain indulgences, one must have at least a general intention to gain them and must in accordance with the tenor of the grant perform the enjoined works at the time and in the manner prescribed.

10) A plenary indulgence can be acquired only once in the course of a day. But one can obtain the plenary indulgence *for the moment of death,* even if another plenary indulgence had already been acquired on the same day. A partial indulgence can be acquired more than once a day, unless otherwise expressly indicated.

11) The work prescribed for acquiring a plenary indulgence connected with a church or oratory consists in a devout visit and the recitation during the visit of one *Our Father* and the *Creed.*

12) To acquire a plenary indulgence it is necessary to perform the work to which the indulgence is attached and to fulfill the following three conditions: Sacramental Confession, Eucharistic Communion, and prayer for the intention of the Sovereign Pontiff. It is further required that all attachment to sin, even venial sin, be absent.

13) The three conditions may be fulfilled several days before or after the performance of the prescribed work; it is, however, fitting that Communion be received and the prayer for the

intention of the Sovereign Pontiff be said on the same day the work is performed.

14) A single Sacramental Confession suffices for gaining several plenary indulgences; but Communion must be received and prayer for the intention of the Sovereign Pontiff must be recited for the gaining of each plenary indulgence.

15) The condition of praying for the intention of the Sovereign Pontiff is fully satisfied by reciting one *Our Father* and one *Hail Mary*; nevertheless, each one is free to recite any other prayer according to his piety and devotion.

16) To gain an indulgence attached to a prayer, it is sufficient to recite the prayer alternately with a companion or to follow it mentally while it is being recited by another.

First General Grant

A PARTIAL indulgence is granted to the faithful who, in the performance of their duties and in bearing the trials of life, raise their mind with humble confidence to God, adding—even if only mentally—some pious invocation.

This first grant is intended to serve as an incentive to the faithful to put into practice the commandment of Christ to "pray always and never lose heart" (Luke 18:1) and at the same time as a reminder so to perform their respective duties as to preserve and strengthen their union with Christ.

Second General Grant

A PARTIAL indulgence is granted to the faithful, who in a spirit of faith and mercy give of themselves or of their goods to serve their brothers in need.

This second grant is intended to serve as an incentive to the faithful to perform more frequent acts of charity and mercy, thus following the example and obeying the command of Christ Jesus (John 13:15; Acts 10:38).

However, not all works of charity are thus indulgenced, but only those that "serve their brothers and sisters in need," in need, for example, of food or clothing for the body or of instruction or comfort for the soul.

Third General Grant

A PARTIAL indulgence Is granted to the faithful, who in a spirit of penance voluntarily deprive themselves of what is licit and pleasing to them.

This third grant is intended to move the faithful to bridle their passions and thus learn to bring their bodies into subjection and to conform themselves to Christ in His poverty and suffering (See Matthew 8:20 and 16: 24).

But self-denial will be more precious, if it is united to charity, according to the teaching of St. Leo the Great: "Let us give to virtue what we refuse to self indulgence. Let what we deny ourselves by fast—be the refreshment of the poor."

Fourth General Grant

A **PARTIAL indulgence Is granted to the faithful, who spontaneously render testimony of faith before others in the particular circumstances of life.**

This concession inspires the faithful to profess the faith before others for the glory of God and the edifice of the Church.

St. Augustine wrote: "May your Creed be for you as a mirror. Look at yourself in it, to see if you believe everything you say you believe. And rejoice in your faith each day" (Sermon 58, 11, 13). "The Christian's everyday life will then be the 'Amen' to the 'I believe' of our baptismal profession of faith (*Catechism of the Catholic Church*, no. 1064).

INDULGENCED WORKS AND PRAYERS

Indulgenced works and prayers ultimately have as their purpose to bring the faithful into a closer union with Christ and the Church through charity. This should also be the basic reason for us to do the work or say the prayer graced with indulgences.

*T*O the four General Grants of indulgences considered above, a few others are here added. These it has seemed beneficial to include, either because of traditional esteem in the case of the old, or because appropriate to the needs of the present in the case of the new.

All these grants complement one another and, while by the offer of an indulgence they move the faithful to perform works of piety, charity, and penance, they at the same time bring them into an ever closer union through charity with Christ the Head and with the Church His body.

The individual works described in the following pages, are each enriched with indulgences. So are the prayers, which merit great respect owing to their Divine inspiration or their antiquity and their more or less universal usage.

Upon close inspection it becomes obvious that these prayers are already included in the First General Grant *mentioned above. For these prayers are recited in the course of their everyday lives by the Christian faithful with hearts raised in humble trust to God. But the Church deemed it helpful to list the prayers separately as being endowed with indulgences in order to eliminate any doubt and* to indicate their prominence.

Wherever a Latin text of a prayer is given in the Enchiridion of Indulgences, *the prayer must be said (in the translation given in the* Enchiridion *or in any approved translation) in order to gain the indulgence. Wherever a prayer is called for but not supplied, any approved prayer with the theme mentioned in the* **Enchiridion** *may be said to gain the indulgence.*

Hence, in this section, a prayer heading without asterisks indicates that the English text that follows is the one given in the **Enchiridion,** *1969 English edition; one asterisk indicates that the prayer that follows is given in the "Supplement" of that edition; two asterisks indicate that the prayer has been supplied for this book and has been approved for the purpose for which it is intended.*

For the complete list of grants, consult the **Enchiridion of Indulgences** *mentioned on p. 9.*

Prayer for All Occasions

DIRECT, we beg You, O Lord,
our actions by Your holy inspirations,
and carry them on by Your gracious assistance,
that every prayer and work of ours may begin
   always with You,
and through You be happily ended.
Amen.

Partial indulgence (no. 1).†

Acts of the Theological Virtues and of Contrition

A partial indulgence is granted to the faithful, who recite devoutly, according to any legitimate formula, the acts of the theological virtues (faith, hope, charity) and of contrition. Each act is indulgenced (no. 2).

---

† A number within parentheses in this section ("Other Grants of Indulgences") indicates the place where the particular prayer is found in the 1969 English edition of the *Enchiridion of Indulgences.*

Act of Faith*

O MY God,
Who are infallible Truth
and can neither
deceive nor be deceived,
I firmly believe all that You have revealed
and propose to my belief through Your holy
    Church,
because You have revealed it.

I believe that You are
one in Nature and three in Persons:
the Father, the Son, and the Holy Spirit.
I believe that You are the Creator of all things
and that You reward the just for all eternity in
    heaven
and punish the wicked for all eternity in hell.

I believe that Jesus Christ is the Son of God
    made man,
that He suffered and died for my sins
and rose from the dead in glory,
and that it is only in Him through the Holy
    Spirit
that eternal life is given to human beings.

I believe in fine all that Your holy Church be-
    lieves.
I thank You for having called me to the true
    Faith,
and I protest that with the help of Your grace
I will live and die in this holy Faith.
Amen.

Act of Hope*†

O MY God,
trusting in Your promises
and because You are faithful, powerful, and merciful,
I hope,
through the merits of Jesus Christ,
for the pardon of my sins,
final perseverance and the blessed glory of heaven.
Amen.

Act of Love*

O MY God,
because You are infinite goodness
and worthy of infinite love,
I love You with my whole heart above all things,
and for love of You I love my neighbors as myself.
Amen.

Act of Contrition*

O MY God,
I repent with my whole heart of all my sins,
and I detest them,
because I have deserved the loss of heaven
and the pains of hell,
but most of all because I have offended You,
infinite Goodness.
I firmly purpose with the help of Your grace,
which I pray You to grant me now and always,

† A single asterisk indicates that the particular prayer is found in the Supplement to the 1969 English edition of the *Enchiridion of Indulgences.*

to do penance
and rather to die than offend You again.
I purpose also to receive the holy Sacraments
during my life and at my death.
Amen.

Adoration of the
Most Blessed Sacrament

A partial indulgence is granted to the faithful, who visit the Most Blessed Sacrament to adore it; a plenary indulgence is granted, if the visit lasts for at least one half an hour (no. 3).

Prayers before the Blessed Sacrament**†

M Y JESUS,
I thank You for having bestowed on me so
many graces:
for having created me,
redeemed me by Your Blood,
made me a Christian by the Sacrament of Baptism,
and borne with me for so long
when I was under Your displeasure.
How unhappy should I be
if I had died in the state of mortal sin!
I should now be lost forever,
O my God,
and I could no longer love You.

I thank You
for having pardoned me in Your mercy,

---

† A double asterisk indicates that the particular prayer was inserted into this section of the 1969 English edition of the *Enchiridion of Indulgences* when it appeared in the *St. Joseph People's Prayer Book,* which received the Imprimatur in 1980.

as I confidently hope.
I thank You especially
for having remained with us in the Blessed
   Sacrament,
for giving Yourself so often to me in Holy Communion,
becoming my food,
and for admitting me now into Your presence.
I thank you for all these favors,
and I hope one day
to thank You more perfectly for them in heaven,
and to celebrate without ceasing Your ineffable
   mercy
for all eternity.
Amen.

Hidden God

HIDDEN God, devoutly I adore You,
   Truly present underneath these veils:
All my heart subdues itself before You,
Since it all before You faints and fails.

Not to sight, or taste, or touch be credit,
Hearing only do we trust secure;
I believe, for God the Son has said it—
Word of Truth that ever shall endure.

On the Cross was veiled Your Godhead's splendor,
Here Your manhood lies hidden too;
Unto both alike my faith I render,
And, as sued the contrite thief, I sue.

Though I look not on Your wounds with Thomas,
You, my Lord, and You, my God, I call:

Make me more and more believe Your promise,
Hope in You, and love You over all.

O memorial of my Savior dying,
Living Bread, that gives life to man;
Make my soul, its life from You supplying,
Taste Your sweetness, as on earth it can.

Deign, O Jesus, Pelican of heaven,
Me, a sinner, in Your Blood to lave,
To a single drop of which is given
All the world from all its sin to save.

Contemplating, Lord, Your hidden presence,
Grant me what I thirst for and implore,
In the revelation of Your essence
To behold Your glory evermore.
Amen.

A partial Indulgence *is granted to the faithful, who recite devoutly the above hymn (no. 4).*

Prayer for Meetings

WE HAVE come,
O Lord, Holy Spirit,
we have come before You,
hampered indeed by our many and grievous sins,
but for a special purpose gathered together in
Your Name.

Come to us
and be with us
and enter our hearts.

Teach us what we are to do
and where we ought to tend;

show us what we must accomplish,
in order that, with Your help,
we may be able to please You in all things.

May You alone be the Author and the Finisher
    of our judgments,
Who alone with God the Father and His Son
possess a glorious Name.

Do not allow us to disturb the order of justice,
You Who love equity above all things.
Let not ignorance draw us into devious paths.
Let not partiality sway our minds
or respect of riches or persons pervert our judg-
    ment.

But unite us to You effectually
by the gift of Your grace alone,
that we may be one in You and never forsake
    the truth;
inasmuch as we are gathered together in Your
    Name,
so may we in all things hold fast to justice tem-
    pered by mercy,
so that in this life
our judgment may in no wise be at variance
    with You
and in the life to come
we may attain to everlasting rewards for deeds
    well done.
Amen.

*This prayer, usually recited at the opening of a meet-
ing to discuss matters of common interest, is enriched
with a* partial indulgence *(no. 5).*

Prayer to St. Joseph

TO you, O blessed Joseph,
do we come in our tribulation,
and having implored the help of your most holy
spouse,
we confidently invoke your patronage also.
Through that charity which bound you
to the immaculate Virgin Mother of God
and through the paternal love
with which you embraced the Child Jesus,
we humbly beg you graciously to regard
the inheritance that Jesus Christ has purchased
by His Blood,
and with your power and strength to aid us in
our necessities.

O most watchful Guardian of the Holy Family,
defend the chosen children of Jesus Christ;
O most loving father,
ward off from us every contagion of error and
corrupting influence;
O our most mighty protector,
be propitious to us and from heaven assist us
in our struggle with the power of darkness;
and, as once you rescued the Child Jesus from
deadly peril,
so now protect God's Holy Church
from the snares of the enemy and from all adversity;
shield, too, each one of us by your constant protection,
so that, supported by your example and your
aid,

we may be able to live piously,
to die holily,
and to obtain eternal happiness in heaven.
Amen.

Partial indulgence (no. 6).

Prayer of Thanksgiving

WE GIVE You thanks, Almighty God,
for all Your blessings:
Who live and reign for ever and ever. Amen.

Partial indulgence (no. 7).

Angel of God

ANGEL of God, my guardian dear,
to whom His love commits me here,
enlighten and guard,
rule and guide me.
Amen.

Partial indulgence (no. 8).

The Angelus

a) *During the year* (outside of Paschal Season)

℣. The Angel of the Lord declared unto Mary,
℟. And she conceived of the Holy Spirit.
Hail Mary.

℣. Behold the handmaid of the Lord,
℟. Be it done unto me according to Your word.
Hail Mary.

℣. And the Word was made flesh,

℟. And dwelt among us.

Hail Mary.

℣. Pray for us, O holy Mother of God,
℟. That we may be made worthy of the promises of Christ.

Let us pray.
Pour forth, we beg You, O Lord,
Your grace into our hearts:
that we, to whom the Incarnation of Christ Your Son
was made known by the message of an Angel,
may by His Passion and Cross
be brought to the glory of His Resurrection.
Through the same Christ our Lord.
Amen.

Queen of Heaven

b) *During Paschal Season*

QUEEN of Heaven, rejoice, alleluia:
For He Whom you merited to bear, alleluia,
Has risen, as He said, alleluia.
Pray for us to God, alleluia.

℣. Rejoice and be glad, O Virgin Mary, alleluia.
℟. Because the Lord is truly risen, alleluia.

Let us pray.
O God, Who by the Resurrection of Your Son, our Lord Jesus Christ,
granted joy to the whole world:
grant, we beg You,

that through the intercession of the Virgin
   Mary, His Mother,
we may lay hold of the joys of eternal life.
Through the same Christ our Lord.
Amen.

*A partial indulgence is granted to the faithful, who
devoutly recite the above prayers according to the formula indicated for the time of the year (no. 9).*

*It is a praiseworthy practice to recite these prayers In
the early morning, at noon, and in the evening.*

Soul of Christ

S OUL of Christ, sanctify me.
   Body of Christ, save me,
Blood of Christ, inebriate.
Water from the side of Christ, wash me.
Passion of Christ, strengthen me.
O good Jesus, hear me.
Within Your wounds, hide me.
Separated from You let me never be.
From the malignant enemy, defend me.
At the hour of death, call me.
To come to You, bid me,
that I may praise You in the company
of Your Saints, for all eternity.
Amen.

Partial indulgence (no. 10).

Papal Blessing

*A plenary indulgence is granted to the faithful, who
piously and devoutly receive, even by radio transmis-
sion, the Blessing of the Sovereign Pontiff, when im-
parted to Rome and the World (no. 12).*

Reception of the Papal Blessing**

MAY the blessing of almighty God:
Father,
Son,
and Holy Spirit,
descend upon You
and remain forever.
℟. Amen.

Act of Spiritual Communion*

An act of spiritual Communion, according to any pious formula, is enriched with a partial indulgence (no. 15).

MY Jesus,
I believe that You are in the Blessed Sacrament.
I love You above all things,
and I long for You in my soul.
Since I cannot now receive You sacramentally,
come at least spiritually into my heart.
As though You have already come,
I embrace You and unite myself entirely to You;
never permit me to be separated from You.
Amen.

The Profession of Faith*

A partial indulgence *is granted to the faithful, who piously recite the Apostles' Creed or the Nicene-Constantinopolitan Creed (no. 16).*

The Apostles' Creed

I BELIEVE in God, the Father almighty,
creator of heaven and earth.

I believe in Jesus Christ, His only Son, our Lord.
He was conceived by the power of the Holy
    Spirit
and born of the Virgin Mary.
He suffered under Pontius Pilate,
was crucified, died, and was buried.
He descended to the dead.
On the third day He rose again.
He ascended into heaven,
and is seated at the right of the Father.
He will come again to judge the living and the
    dead.
I believe in the Holy Spirit,
the holy Catholic Church,
the Communion of Saints,
the forgiveness of sins,
the resurrection of the body,
and the life everlasting.
Amen.

The Nicene Creed

WE believe in one God,
    the Father, the Almighty,
maker of heaven and earth,
of all that is seen and unseen.   *Visable & invisable*

We believe in one Lord, Jesus Christ,
the only Son of God,
eternally begotten of the Father,
God from God, Light from Light,
true God from true God,
begotten, not made, one in Being with the
    Father.   *Consstantial*

Through Him all things were made.
For us and for our salvation
He came down from heaven:

All bow at the following words up to: and became
man.

by the power of the Holy Spirit
He was born of the Virgin Mary, and became
man.
For our sake He was crucified under Pontius
Pilate;
He suffered, died, and was buried.
On the third day He rose again
in ~~fulfillment~~ of the Scriptures; *accordance*
He ascended into heaven
and is seated at the right hand of the Father.
He will come again in glory to judge the living
and the dead,
and His kingdom will have no end.

We believe in the Holy Spirit, the Lord, the
giver of life,
Who proceeds from the Father and the Son.
With the Father and the Son He is worshiped
and glorified.
He has spoken through the Prophets.
We believe in one holy Catholic and apostolic
Church
We acknowledge one Baptism for the forgive-
ness of sins.
We look for the resurrection of the dead,
and the life of the world to come.
Amen.

Psalm 130—The De Profundis

A partial indulgence *is granted to the faithful, who piously recite the psalm* Out of the depths (Psalm 130) (no. 19).

Prayer for Pardon and Peace

Plea to be heard

OUT of the depths I cry to You, O Lord;
O Lord, hear my voice.
Let Your ears to be attentive
to my cries of supplication.

God's pardon

If You, O Lord, kept a record of our sins,
O Lord, who could stand upright?
But with You there is forgiveness
so that You may be revered.

Trust in God's mercy

I wait for the Lord in anxious expectation;
I place my hope in His word.
My soul waits for the Lord
more than watchmen wait for the dawn.

Hope in the Redemption

More than watchmen wait for the dawn
let Israel wait for the Lord.
For with the Lord there is kindness,
as well as plenteous redemption.
He alone will redeem Israel
from all its sins.

Psalm-prayer

God, You are power and life.
In the Incarnation of Your Son

You stooped down to us sinners
and raised us from the depths of our sinfulness.
Strengthen Your Church
that she may live with confidence in Your salvation. Amen.

Christian Doctrine

A partial indulgence *is granted to the faithful, who
take part in teaching or in learning Christian doctrine.*

*N.B.: One who in a spirit of faith and charity teaches
Christian doctrine can gain a* partial indulgence *according to the second of the four general grants of indulgences; see above, p. 14.*

This new grant confirms the partial indulgence *in
favor of the teacher of Christian doctrine and extends it
to the learner (no. 20).*

Prayer for Those Who Study
or Teach Christian Doctrine**

L ORD Jesus Christ,
   by Your Holy Spirit
You give to some the word of wisdom,
to others the word of knowledge,
and to still others the word of faith.
Grant us a knowledge of the Father
and of Yourself.

Help us to cling steadfastly
to the Catholic Faith.
In our studies and in our teaching
make us seek only the extension of Your Kingdom
and Your holy Church
both in ourselves and in others.
Amen.

Prayer at the Beginning of the Day

L ORD, God Almighty,
   You have brought us safely to the beginning
   of this day.
Defend us today by Your mighty power,
that we may not fall into any sin,
but that all our words may so proceed
and all our thoughts and actions be so directed,
as to be always just in Your sight.
Through Christ our Lord.
Amen.

Partial indulgence (no. 21).

Prayer before a Crucifix

L OOK down upon me,
   good and gentle Jesus,
while before Your face I humbly kneel,
and with burning soul pray and beseech You
to fix deep in my heart
lively sentiments of faith, hope, and charity,
true contrition for my sins,
and a firm purpose of amendment,
while I contemplate with great love and tender
   pity
Your five wounds,
pondering over them within me,
calling to mind the words that David, Your
   Prophet,
said of You, my good Jesus:
"They have pierced My hands and My feet;
they have numbered all my bones" (Psalm
   22:17-18).
Amen.

A plenary indulgence *is granted on each Friday of Lent to the faithful, who after Communion piously recite the above prayer before an image of Christ crucified; on other days of the year the indulgence* is partial *(no. 22).*

Eucharistic Congress

A plenary indulgence *is granted to the faithful, who devoutly participate in the customary solemn Eucharistic Rite at the close of a Eucharistic Congress (no. 27).*

Prayer for a Eucharistic Congress**

O JESUS,
You are really present in the Blessed Sacrament
to be our spiritual food and drink.
Bless and bring to a successful issue
all Eucharistic congresses,
especially this one.

Enkindle the hearts of priests and faithful
so that frequent and daily Communion may be held in honor
in all the countries of the world.
May Your Kingship over human society
be everywhere acknowledged.
Amen.

Prayer for the Household

HEAR us,
Lord, holy Father, almighty and eternal God;
and graciously send Your holy Angel from heaven

to watch over, to cherish, to protect,
to abide with, and to defend
all who dwell in this house.
Through Christ our Lord. Amen.

Partial indulgence (no. 24).

Retreats

A plenary indulgence *is granted to the faithful, who
spend at least three whole days in the spiritual exercises
of a retreat (no. 25).*

Prayer for the Success
of Retreats**

O JESUS,
our Redeemer and our King,
during these spiritual exercises
Your representatives will break for us
the bread of God's Word
and bring us the joy of forgiveness.
Help all who make this retreat
to be faithful to Your grace
and respond generously to Your mercy.
Let the preaching of Your eternal truths
enlighten our minds
and move our hearts
so that we may realize our shortcomings
and sincerely repent of them.

For a prayer after a retreat, see p. 70.

Act of Reparation to the Sacred Heart

MOST sweet Jesus,
   Whose overflowing charity for human
      beings is requited
by so much forgetfulness, negligence, and contempt,
behold us prostrate before You,
eager to repair by a special act of homage
the cruel indifference and injuries
to which Your loving Heart is everywhere
   subject.

Mindful, alas! that we ourselves have had a
   share
in such great indignities,
which we now deplore from the depths of our
   hearts,
we humbly ask Your pardon
and declare our readiness to atone by voluntary
   expiation,
not only for our own personal offenses
but also for the sins of those who,
straying far from the path of salvation,
refuse in their obstinate infidelity to follow You,
their Shepherd and Leader,
or, renouncing the promises of their Baptism,
have cast off the yoke of Your law.

We are now resolved to expiate
each and every deplorable outrage committed
   against You;
we are now determined to make amends
for the manifold offenses against Christian
   modesty

in unbecoming dress and behavior,
for all the foul seductions laid
to ensnare the feet of the innocent,
for the frequent violations of Sundays and holy-
days,
and the shocking blasphemies uttered against
You
and Your Saints.

We wish also to make amends for the insults
to which Your Vicar on earth and Your priests
are subjected,
for the profanation,
by conscious neglect or terrible acts of sacrilege,
of the very Sacrament of Your Divine love,
and lastly for the public crimes of nations
who resist the rights and teaching authority of
the Church
that You have founded.

Would that we were able
to wash away such abominations with our
blood.
We now offer,
in reparation for these violations of Your Divine
honor,
the satisfaction You once made
to Your Eternal Father on the Cross
and that You continue to renew daily on our
altars;
we offer it in union with the acts of atonement
of Your Virgin Mother and all the Saints
and of the pious faithful on earth;
and we sincerely promise to make recompense,

as far as we can with the help of Your grace,
for all neglect of Your great love
and for the sins we and others have committed.
Henceforth, we will live a life of unswerving faith,
of purity of conduct,
of perfect observance of the precepts of the Gospel
and especially that of charity.
We promise to the best of our power
to prevent others from offending You
and to bring as many as possible to follow You.

O loving Jesus,
through the intercession of the Blessed Virgin Mother,
our model in reparation,
deign to receive the voluntary offering we make
of this act of expiation;
and by the crowning gift of perseverance
keep us faithful unto death
in our duty and the allegiance we owe to You,
so that we may all one day come to that happy home,
where with the Father and the Holy Spirit
You live and reign, God,
forever and ever.
Amen.

A partial indulgence *is granted to the faithful, who piously recite the above act of reparation. A* plenary indulgence *is granted if it is publicly recited on the feast of the Most Sacred Heart of Jesus (no. 26).*

Act of Dedication to Christ the King

MOST sweet Jesus,
Redeemer of the human race,
look down upon us humbly prostrate before
  You.
We are Yours, and Yours we wish to be;
but to be more surely united with You,
behold, we freely consecrate ourselves today
to Your Most Sacred Heart.
Many indeed have never known You;
many, too, despising Your precepts,
have rejected You.
Have mercy on them all, most merciful Jesus,
and draw them to Your Sacred Heart.

Be King, O Lord,
not only of the faithful who have never forsaken
  You
but also of the prodigal children who have
  abandoned You;
grant that they may quickly return to their
  Father's house,
lest they die of wretchedness and hunger.

Be King of those who are deceived by erroneous
  opinions,
or whom discord keeps aloof,
and call them back to the harbor of truth
and the unity of faith,
so that soon there may be but one flock and one
  Shepherd.

Grant, O Lord, to Your Church

assurance of freedom and immunity from harm;

give tranquility of order to all nations;

make the earth resound from pole to pole with one cry:

Praise to the Divine Heart that wrought our salvation;

to It be glory and honor forever.

Amen.

A partial indulgence *is granted to the faithful, who piously recite the above Act of Dedication of the Human Race to Jesus Christ King. A* plenary indulgence *is granted, if it is recited publicly on the feast of our Lord Jesus Christ King (no. 27).*

At the Approach of Death

To the faithful in danger of death, who cannot be assisted by a priest to bring them the Sacraments and impart the Apostolic Blessing with its plenary indulgence, Holy Mother Church nevertheless grants a plenary indulgence *to be acquired at the point of death, provided they are properly disposed and have been in the habit of reciting some prayers during their lifetime. The use of a crucifix or a cross to gain this indulgence is praiseworthy.*

The condition: provided they have been in the habit of reciting some prayers during their lifetime *supplies in such cases for the three usual conditions required for the gaining of a plenary indulgence.*

The plenary indulgence at the point of death can be acquired by the faithful, even if they have already obtained another plenary indulgence on the same day (no. 28).

Prayer for a Good Death**

O JESUS,
while I adore Your dying breath,
I beg You to receive mine.
Since I do not know
whether I shall have command of my senses
when I depart from this world,
I offer You even now my last agony
and all the sorrows of my passing.
I give my soul into Your hands
for You are my Father and my Savior.
Grant that the last beat of my heart
may be an act of perfect love for You.
Amen.

Litanies

The following Litanies are each enriched with a partial indulgence: *the Most Holy Name of Jesus, the Most Sacred Heart of Jesus, the Most Precious Blood of our Lord Jesus Christ, the Blessed Virgin Mary, St. Joseph, and the Saints (no. 29).*

Litany of the Most Holy Name of Jesus*

L ORD, have mercy.
Christ, have mercy.
Lord, have mercy.
Jesus, hear us.
Jesus, graciously hear us.
God, the Father of heaven,
    have mercy on us.†
God the Son, Redeemer of the world,
God, the Holy Spirit,

Holy Trinity, one God,
Jesus Son of the living God,
Jesus, splendor of the Father,
Jesus, brightness of eternal light,
Jesus, King of glory,
Jesus, Sun of justice,
Jesus, Son of the Virgin Mary,

† Have mercy on us *is repeated after each invocation.*

Jesus, most amiable,

Jesus, most admirable,

Jesus, the mighty God,

Jesus, Father of the world to come,

Jesus, Angel of great counsel,

Jesus, most powerful,

Jesus, most patient,

Jesus, most obedient,

Jesus, meek and humble of heart,

Jesus, lover of chastity,

Jesus, our lover,

Jesus, God of peace,

Jesus, author of life,

Jesus, model of virtues,

Jesus, zealous for souls,

Jesus, our God,

Jesus, our refuge,

Jesus, father of the poor,

Jesus, treasure of the faithful,

Jesus, good shepherd,

Jesus, true light,

Jesus, eternal wisdom,

Jesus, infinite goodness,

Jesus, our way and our life,

Jesus, joy of the Angels,

Jesus, king of the Patriarchs,

Jesus, master of the Apostles,

Jesus, teacher of the Evangelists,

Jesus, strength of Martyrs,

Jesus, light of Confessors,

Jesus, purity of Virgins,

Jesus, crown of all Saints,

Be merciful, *spare us, O Jesus!*

Be merciful, *graciously hear us, O Jesus!*

From all evil, *deliver us, O Jesus!*†

From all sin,

From Your wrath,

From the snares of the devil,

From the spirit of fornication,

From everlasting death,

From the neglect of Your inspirations,

Through the mystery of Your holy Incarnation,

Through Your Nativity,

Through Your Infancy,

Through Your most Divine Life,

Through Your Labors,

Through Your Agony and Passion,

Through Your Cross and Dereliction,

Through Your Sufferings,

Through Your Death and Burial,

Through Your Resurrection,

Through Your Ascension,

Through Your Institution of the most holy Eucharist,

Through Your Joys,

Through Your Glory,

Lamb of God, You take

† Deliver us, O Jesus, *is repeated after each invocation.*

away the sins of the world; *spare us, O Jesus!*
Lamb of God, You take away the sins of the world; *graciously hear us, O Jesus!*

Lamb of God, You take away the sins of the world, *have mercy on us, O Jesus!*
℣. Jesus, hear us.
℞. *Jesus, graciously hear us.*

L ET us pray.
O Lord Jesus Christ, You have said,
"Ask and You shall receive;
seek, and You shall find;
knock, and it shall be opened to You";
mercifully attend to our supplications,
and grant us the grace of Your most Divine love,
that we may love You with all our hearts,
and in all our words and actions,
and never cease to praise You.

Make us, O Lord,
to have a perpetual fear and love of Your holy Name,
for You never fail to govern
those whom You solidly establish in Your love.
You Who live and reign forever and ever.
℞. **Amen.**

Litany of the Most Sacred Heart of Jesus*

L ORD, have mercy.
Christ, have mercy.
Lord, have mercy.
Christ, hear us.
Christ, graciously hear us.

God, the Father of heaven, *have mercy on us.*†
God the Son, Redeemer of the world,
God, the Holy Spirit,

† Have mercy on us *is repeated after each invocation.*

Holy Trinity, one God,

Heart of Jesus, Son of the eternal Father,

Heart of Jesus, formed by the Holy Spirit in the womb of the Virgin Mother,

Heart of Jesus, substantially united to the Word of God,

Heart of Jesus, of infinite majesty,

Heart of Jesus, sacred temple of God,

Heart of Jesus, tabernacle of the Most High,

Heart of Jesus, house of God and gate of heaven,

Heart of Jesus, burning furnace of charity,

Heart of Jesus, abode of justice and love,

Heart of Jesus, full of goodness and love,

Heart of Jesus, abyss of all virtues,

Heart of Jesus, most worthy of all praise,

Heart of Jesus, King and center of all hearts,

Heart of Jesus, in Whom are all the treasures of wisdom and knowledge,

Heart of Jesus, in Whom dwells the fullness of Divinity,

Heart of Jesus, in Whom the Father was well pleased,

Heart of Jesus, of Whose fullness we have all received,

Heart of Jesus, desire of the everlasting hills,

Heart of Jesus, patient and most merciful,

Heart of Jesus, enriching all who invoke You,

Heart of Jesus, fountain of life and holiness,

Heart of Jesus, propitiation for our sins,

Heart of Jesus, loaded down with opprobrium,

Heart of Jesus, bruised for our offenses,

Heart of Jesus, obedient to death,

Heart of Jesus, pierced with a lance,

Heart of Jesus, source of all consolation,

Heart of Jesus, our life and resurrection,

Heart of Jesus, our peace and reconciliation,

Heart of Jesus, victim for our sins,

Heart of Jesus, salvation of those who trust in You,

Heart of Jesus, hope of those who die in You,

Heart of Jesus, delight of all the Saints,

Lamb of God, You take away the sins of the world; *spare us, O Lord!*

Lamb of God, You take away the sins of the world; *graciously hear us, O Lord!*

Lamb of God, You take away the sins of the world; *have mercy on us.*

℣. Jesus, meek and humble of heart.

℟. *Make our hearts like to Yours.*

L ET us pray.
Almighty and eternal God,
look upon the Heart of Your most beloved Son
and upon the praises and satisfaction
that He offers You in the name of sinners;
and to those who implore Your mercy,
in Your great goodness, grant forgiveness
in the Name of the same Jesus Christ, Your Son,
Who lives and reigns with You forever and ever.
℟. Amen.

Litany of the Most Precious Blood of Jesus*

L ORD, have mercy.
Christ have mercy

Lord, have mercy.

Christ, hear us.

Christ, graciously hear us.

God, the Father of heaven, *have mercy on us.*

God the Son, Redeemer of the world, *have mercy on us.*

God, the Holy Spirit, *have mercy on us.*

Holy Trinity, one God, *have mercy on us.*

Blood of Christ, only-begotten Son of the eternal Father, save us.†

Blood of Christ, Incarnate Word of God,

Blood of Christ, of the New and Eternal Testament,

Blood of Christ, falling upon the earth in the Agony,

† Save us *is repeated after each invocation.*

Blood of Christ, shed profusely in the Scourging,

Blood of Christ, flowing forth in the Crowning with Thorns,

Blood of Christ, poured out on the Cross,

Blood of Christ, price of our salvation,

Blood of Christ, without which there is no forgiveness,

Blood of Christ, Eucharistic drink and refreshment of souls,

Blood of Christ, stream of mercy,

Blood of Christ, victor over demons,

Blood of Christ, courage of Martyrs,

Blood of Christ, strength of Confessors,

Blood of Christ, bringing forth Virgins,

Blood of Christ, help of those in peril,

Blood of Christ, relief of the burdened,

Blood of Christ, solace in sorrow,

Blood of Christ, hope of the penitent,

Blood of Christ, consolation of the dying,

Blood of Christ, peace and tenderness of hearts,

Blood of Christ, pledge of eternal life,

Blood of Christ, freeing souls from purgatory,

Blood of Christ, most worthy of all glory and honor,

Lamb of God, You take away the sins of the world; *spare us, O Lord!*

Lamb of God, You take away the sins of the world; *graciously hear us, O Lord!*

Lamb of God, You take away the sins of the world: *have mercy on us.*

℣. You have redeemed us, O Lord, in Your Blood.

℟. *And made us, for our God, a kingdom.*

L ET us pray.
Almighty and eternal God,
You have appointed Your only-begotten Son
the Redeemer of the world,
and willed to be appeased by His Blood.
Grant, we beg of You,
that we may worthily adore this price of our salvation,

and through Its power
be safeguarded from the evils of the present life,
so that we may rejoice in Its fruits forever in
   heaven.
Through the same Christ our Lord.
℟. Amen.

Litany of the Blessed Virgin Mary*

L ORD, have mercy.
   Christ, have mercy.
Lord, have mercy.
Christ, hear us.
Christ, graciously hear us.
God, the Father of heaven,
   have mercy on us.
God the Son, Redeemer of
   the world, *have mercy on
   us.*
God the Holy Spirit, *have
   mercy on us.*
Holy Trinity, one God, *have
   mercy on us.*
Holy Mary, pray for us. †
Holy Mother of God,
Holy Virgin of virgins,
Mother of Christ,
Mother of the Church,
Mother of Divine grace,
Mother most pure,
Mother most chaste,
Mother inviolate,
Mother undefiled,
Mother most amiable,
Mother most admirable,
Mother of good counsel,
Mother of our Creator,
Mother of our Savior,
Virgin most prudent,
Virgin most venerable,
Virgin most renowned,
Virgin most powerful,
Virgin most merciful,
Virgin most faithful,
Mirror of justice,
Seat of wisdom,
Cause of our joy,
Spiritual vessel,
Vessel of honor,
Singular vessel of devo-
   tion,
Mystical rose,
Tower of David,
Tower of ivory,
House of gold,
Ark of the covenant,
Gate of heaven,
Morning star,
Health of the sick,
Refuge of sinners,
Comforter of the afflicted,
Help of Christians,
Queen of Angels,

† Pray for us *is repeated after each invocation.*

Queen, of Patriarchs,
Queen of Prophets,
Queen of Apostles,
Queen of Martyrs,
Queen of Confessors,
Queen of Virgins,
Queen of all Saints,
Queen conceived without original sin,
Queen assumed into heaven,
Queen of the most holy Rosary,
Queen of families,
Queen of peace,

Lamb of God, You take away the sins of the world; *spare us, O Lord!*

Lamb of God, You take away the sins of the world; *graciously hear us, O Lord!*

Lamb of God, You take away the sins of the world; *have mercy on us.*

℣. Pray for us, O holy Mother of God.

℟. *That we may be made worthy of the promises of Christ.*

L ET us pray.
Grant, we beg You, O Lord God,
that we Your servants
may enjoy lasting health of mind and body,
and by the glorious intercession
of the Blessed Mary, ever Virgin,
be delivered from present sorrow
and enter into the joy of eternal happiness.
Through Christ our Lord.
℟. Amen.

During Advent

L ET us pray.
O God,
You willed that, at the message of an Angel,
Your Word should take flesh
in the womb of the Blessed Virgin Mary;
grant to Your suppliant people,

that we, who believe her to be truly the Mother
    of God.
may be helped by her intercession with You.
Through the same Christ our Lord.
℟. Amen.

From Christmas to the Purification

L ET us pray.
    O God,
by the fruitful virginity of Blessed Mary,
You bestowed upon the human race
the rewards of eternal salvation;
grant, we beg You,
that we may feel the power of her intercession,
through whom we have been made worthy
to receive the Author of life,
our Lord Jesus Christ Your Son,
Who lives and reigns with You forever and ever.
℟. Amen.

During Paschaltime

L ET us pray.
    O God,
Who by the Resurrection of Your Son,
our Lord Jesus Christ,
granted joy to the whole world,
grant, we beg You,
that through the intercession of the Virgin
    Mary, His Mother,
we may attain the joys of eternal life.
Through the same Christ our Lord.
℟. Amen.

Litany of St. Joseph*

L ORD, have mercy.
Christ, have mercy.
Lord, have mercy.
Christ, hear us.
Christ, graciously hear us.
God, the Father of Heaven, *have mercy on us.*
God the Son, Redeemer of the world, *have mercy on us.*
God the Holy Spirit, *have mercy on us.*
Holy Trinity, one God, *have mercy on us.*
Holy Mary, *pray for us.*†
St. Joseph,
Renowned offspring of David,
Light of Patriarchs,
Spouse of the Mother of God,
Chaste guardian of the Virgin,
Foster father of the Son of God,
Diligent protector of Christ,
Head of the Holy Family,
Joseph most just,
Joseph most chaste,

Joseph most prudent,
Joseph most strong,
Joseph most obedient,
Joseph most faithful,
Mirror of patience,
Lover of poverty,
Model of artisans,
Glory of home life,
Guardian of virgins,
Pillar of families,
Solace of the wretched,
Hope of the sick,
Patron of the dying,
Terror of demons,
Protector of Holy Church,
Lamb of God, You take away the sins of the world; *spare us, O Lord!*
Lamb of God, You take away the sins of the world; *graciously hear us, O Lord!*
Lamb of God, You take away the sins of the world; *have mercy on us.*
℣. He made him the lord of His household.
℟. *And prince over all His possessions.*

L ET us pray.
O God,
in Your ineffable providence
You were pleased to choose Blessed Joseph
to be the spouse of Your most holy Mother;

† Pray for us *is repeated after each invocation.*

grant, we beg You,
that we may be worthy
to have him for our intercessor in heaven
whom on earth we venerate as our Protector:
You Who live and reign forever and ever.
℞. Amen.

Litany of the Saints*

LORD, have mercy.
Christ, have mercy.
Lord, have mercy.
Christ, hear us.
Christ, graciously hear us.
God the Father of Heaven,
have mercy on us.
God the Son, Redeemer of
the world,
have mercy on us.
God the Holy Spirit,
have mercy on us.
Holy Trinity, one God,
have mercy on us.
Holy Mary, *pray for us.*†
Holy Mother of God,
Holy Virgin of virgins,
St. Michael,
St. Gabriel,
St. Raphael,
All you holy Angels and
Archangels,
All you holy orders of
blessed spirits,
St. John the Baptist,
St. Joseph,

All you holy Patriarchs and
Prophets,
St. Peter,
St. Paul,
St. Andrew,
St. James
St. John,
St. Thomas,
St. James,
St. Philip,
St. Bartholomew,
St. Matthew,
St. Simon,
St. Thaddeus,
St. Matthias,
St. Barnabas,
St. Luke,
St. Mark,
All you holy Apostles and
Evangelists,
All you holy Disciples of the
Lord,
All you holy Innocents,
St. Stephen,
St. Lawrence,
St. Vincent,
Sts. Fabian and Sebastian,

† Pray for us *is repeated after each invocation down to*
All you holy Virgins and Widows.

Sts. John and Paul,

Sts. Cosmas and Damian,

Sts. Gervase and Protase,

All you holy Martyrs,

St. Sylvester,

St. Gregory,

St. Ambrose,

St. Augustine,

St. Jerome,

St. Martin,

St. Nicholas,

All you holy Bishops and Confessors,

All you holy Doctors,

St. Anthony,

St. Benedict,

St. Bernard,

St. Dominic,

St. Francis,

All you holy Priests and Levites,

All you holy Monks and Hermits,

St. Mary Magdalene,

St. Agatha,

St. Lucy,

St. Agnes,

St. Cecilia,

St. Catherine,

St. Anastasia,

All you holy Virgins and Widows,

All you holy Men and Women, Saints of God, *make intercession for us.*

Be merciful, *spare us, O Lord.*

Be merciful, *graciously hear us, O Lord.*

From all evil, O Lord, *deliver us.*†

From all sin,

From Your wrath,

From sudden and unprovided death,

From the snares of the devil,

From anger, and hatred, and all ill-will,

From the spirit of fornication,

From lightning and tempest,

From the scourge of earthquake,

From plague, famine, and war,

From everlasting death,

Through the mystery of Your holy Incarnation,

Through Your Coming,

Through Your Nativity,

Through Your Baptism and holy Fasting,

Through Your Cross and Passion,

Through Your Death and Burial,

Through Your holy Resurrection,

Through Your admirable Ascension,

Through the coming of the Holy Spirit, the Paraclete,

† O Lord, deliver us *is repeated down to* In the day of judgment.

In the day of judgment,

We sinners, *we beseech You, hear us.* †

That You would spare us.

That You would pardon us,

That You would bring us to true penance,

That You would deign to govern and preserve Your holy Church,

That You would deign to preserve our Apostolic Prelate, and all orders of the Church in holy religion,

That You would deign to humble the enemies of Holy Church,

That You would deign to give peace and true concord to Christian kings and princes,

That You would deign to grant peace and unity to all Christian people,

That You would deign to call back to the unity of the Church all who have strayed from the truth and lead all unbelievers to the light of the Gospel,

That You would deign to confirm and preserve us in Your holy service,

That You would lift up our minds to heavenly desires,

That You would render eternal blessings to all our benefactors,

That You would deliver our souls and the souls of our brethren, relations, and benefactors, from eternal damnation,

That You would deign to give and preserve the fruits of the earth,

That You would deign to grant eternal rest to all the faithful departed,

That You would deign graciously to hear us,

Son of God,

Lamb of God, You take away the sins of the world; *spare us, O Lord!*

Lamb of God, You take away the sins of the world; *graciously hear us, O Lord!*

Lamb of God, You take away the sins of the world; *have mercy on us.*

Christ, hear us,

Christ, graciously hear us.

Lord, have mercy.

Christ, have mercy.

Lord, have mercy.

Our Father, etc. (inaudibly).

℣. And lead us not into temptation.

℟. *But deliver us from evil.*

† We beseech You, hear us *is repeated down to* Son of God.

PSALM 70

DEIGN, O God, to rescue me;
O Lord, make haste to help me.
Let them be put to shame and confounded
who seek my life.
Let them be turned back in disgrace
who desire my ruin.
Let them retire in their shame
who say to me, "Aha, aha!"
But may all who seek You exult
and be glad in You,
And may those who love Your salvation
say ever, "God be glorified!"
But I am afflicted and poor;
O God, hasten to me!
You are my help and my deliverer;
O Lord, hold not back!
Glory be to the Father, and to the Son,
and to the Holy Spirit.
As it was in the beginning, is now, and ever shall be,
world without end. Amen

℣. Save Your servants,
℟. *Who trust in You, O my God.*
℣. Be a tower of strength for us, O Lord,
℟. *Against the attack of the enemy.*

℣. Let not the enemy prevail against us.
℟. *And let not the son of evil dare to harm us.*
℣. O Lord, deal not with us according to our sins.
℟. *Neither requite us according to our iniquities.*
℣. Let us pray for our Sovereign Pontiff N.
℟. *The Lord preserve him, and give him life, and make him blessed upon the earth, and deliver him not up to the will of his enemies.*
℣. Let us pray for our benefactors.
℟. *Deign, O Lord, for Your name's sake, to reward with eternal life all those who do us good. Amen.*
℣. Let us pray for the faithful departed.
℟. *Eternal rest give to them, O Lord; and let perpetual light shine upon them.*
℣. May they rest in peace.
℟. *Amen.*
℣. For our absent brethren.
℟. *Save Your servants, who trust in You, my God.*
℣. Send them help, O Lord, from Your sanctuary.
℟. *And sustain them from Zion.*
℣. O Lord, hear my prayer.

R̷. *And let my cry come to You.* | V̷. The Lord be with you.
R̷. *And with your spirit.*

L ET us pray.
O God,
Whose property is always to have mercy and to
  spare,
receive our petition, that we,
and all Your servants who are bound by the
  chains of sin,
may, by the compassion of Your goodness,
be mercifully absolved.

G RACIOUSLY hear,
we beg You, O Lord,
the prayers of Your suppliants,
and pardon the sins of those who confess to
  You,
that in Your bounty
You may grant us both pardon and peace.

I N YOUR clemency, O Lord,
show us Your ineffable mercy,
that You may both free us from all our sins,
and deliver us from the punishments
that we deserve for them.

O GOD,
Who by sin are offended and by penance
  pacified,
mercifully regard the prayers of Your suppliant
  people,

and turn away the scourges of Your anger,
that we deserve for our sins.

ALMIGHTY, everlasting God,
have mercy upon Your servant N., our
Sovereign Pontiff,
and direct him according to Your clemency
into the way of everlasting salvation,
that by Your grace
he may desire those things that are pleasing to
You,
and perform them with all his strength.

O GOD,
from Whom are holy desires,
good counsels, and just works,
give to Your servants
that peace which the world cannot give,
that our hearts may be set to keep Your commandments,
and that, being removed from the fear of our
enemies,
we may pass our time in peace under Your protection.

BURN our desires and our hearts
with the fire of the Holy Spirit,
O Lord,
that we may serve You with a chaste body,
and with a clean heart be pleasing to You.

O GOD, the Creator and Redeemer of all the
faithful,
grant to the souls of Your servants and hand-
maids

the remission of all their sins,
that, through devout prayers,
they may obtain the pardon that they always
  desired.

D IRECT, we beg You, O Lord,
  our actions by Your holy inspirations,
and carry them on by Your gracious assistance,
that every prayer and work of ours
may begin always with You,
and through You be happily ended.

A LMIGHTY and everlasting God,
  You have dominion over the living and the
  dead,
and You are merciful to all who You foreknow
will be Yours by faith and good works;
we humbly beg You
that those for whom we intend to pour forth our
  prayers,
whether this present world still detain them in
  the flesh,
or the world to come has already received them
out of their bodies,
may, through the intercession of all Your Saints,
by the clemency of Your goodness,
obtain the remission of all their sins.
Through Christ our Lord.
℟. *Amen.*
℣. O Lord, hear my prayer.
℟. *And let my cry come to You.*
℣. May the almighty and merciful Lord graciously hear us.

℞. *Amen.*

℣. And may the souls of the faithful departed, through the mercy of God, rest in peace.

℞. *Amen.*

Magnificat

A partial indulgence *is granted to the faithful, who piously recite the canticle of the Magnificat (no. 30).*

Canticle of Mary

The Soul Rejoices in the Lord

MY SOUL proclaims the greatness of the Lord; my spirit finds its joy in God my Savior.

For He has looked upon His handmaid in her lowliness;

all future generations shall call me blessed.

God Who is all-powerful has done wondrous deeds for me,

and blessed is His Name.

His mercy has been shown throughout every age to those who fear Him.

The Lord has shown great power with His arm;

He has bewildered the proud in their inmost thoughts.

He has unseated the mighty from their thrones and raised up the lowly.

The hungry He has provided with every choice food

while the rich He has sent away unfed.

He has given unfailing support to Israel His servant,

always mindful of His mercy,
as He promised our fathers,
promised Abraham and His descendants for-
ever.   Luke 1:46-55

A Child's Prayer to Mary

MARY, Mother of grace,
Mother of mercy,
Shield me from the enemy
And receive me at the hour of my death.
Amen.

Partial indulgence (no. 31).

The Memorare

REMEMBER, O most gracious Virgin Mary,
that never was it known
that anyone who fled to your protection,
implored your help or sought your intercession,
was left unaided.
Inspired with this confidence,
I fly to you, O Virgin of virgins, my Mother;
to you do I come,
before you I stand, sinful and sorrowful.
O Mother of the Word Incarnate,
despise not my petitions,
but in your mercy hear and answer me.
Amen.

Partial indulgence (no. 32).

Psalm 51—The Miserere

A partial indulgence is granted to the faithful, who with repentant heart recite Ps 51 (vv. 3-21) (no. 33).

Prayer before Confession

Sincere sorrow for sin

HAVE mercy on me, O God,
in accord with Your kindness;
in Your abundant compassion
wipe away my offenses.
Wash me completely from my guilt,
and cleanse me from my sin.

For I am fully aware of my offense,
and my sin is ever before me.
Against You, You alone, have I sinned;
I have done what is evil in Your sight.

Therefore, You are right in accusing me
and just in passing judgment.
Indeed, I was born in iniquity,
and in sin did my mother conceive me.

But You desire sincerity of heart;
and You endow my innermost being with
wisdom.
Sprinkle me with hyssop so that I may be
cleansed;
wash me until I am whiter than snow.

Let me experience joy and gladness;
let the bones You have crushed exult.
Hide Your face from my sins,
and wipe out all my offenses.

Create in me a clean heart, O God,
and renew a resolute spirit within me.
Do not cast me out from Your presence
or take away from me Your Holy Spirit.

Restore to me the joy of being saved,
and grant me the strength of a generous spirit.

Praise of God for His mercy

I will teach Your ways to the wicked,
and sinners will return to You.

Deliver me from bloodguilt, O God,
the God of my salvation,
and I will proclaim Your righteousness.
O Lord, open my lips,
and my mouth will proclaim Your praise.

For You take no delight in sacrifice;
if I were to make a burnt offering,
You would refuse to accept it.
My sacrifice, O God, is a broken spirit;
a contrite and humble heart, O God,
You will not spurn.

In Your kindness, deal favorably with Zion;
build up the walls of Jerusalem.
Then You will delight in righteous sacrifices,
in burnt offerings and whole oblations,
and young bulls will be offered on Your altar.

Psalm-prayer

Merciful God,
that we might become the very holiness of God,
You made Your Son Who did not know sin
to be sin.
Consider our repentance
and raise us up in Your goodness,
that we may sing Your praise and Your glory
in the Holy Spirit before the nations.
Amen.

Novena Devotions

A partial indulgence is granted to the faithful, who devoutly take part in the pious exercises of a public novena before the feast of Christmas or Pentecost or the Immaculate Conception of the Blessed Virgin Mary (no. 34).

Prayer for Novena Devotions
(Christmas)**

GOD of love, Father of all,
the darkness that covered the earth
has given way to the bright dawn
of Your Word made flesh.
Make us a people of this light.
Make us faithful to Your Word,
that we may bring Your life
to the waiting world.
Amen.

Use of Articles of Devotion

The faithful, who devoutly use an article of devotion (crucifix or cross, rosary, scapular or medal) properly blessed by any priest, obtain a partial indulgence.

But if the article of devotion has been blessed by the Sovereign Pontiff or by any Bishop, the faithful, using it, can also gain, a plenary indulgence on the feast of the Holy Apostles, Peter and Paul, provided they also make a profession of faith according to any legitimate formula (no. 35).

Prayer While Using an Article
of Devotion**

FATHER in heaven,
we give You thanks for sending Your Spirit
to teach us to pray.

Bless this article of devotion
and let it become for us
an aid to sincere and devout prayer.
May we become daily more proficient in prayer
and more pleasing to You.

Prayer for Priestly or Religious Vocations

A partial indulgence is granted to the faithful, who recite a prayer, approved by ecclesiastical Authority, for the above intention (no. 37).

Prayer for Priestly Vocations**

O JESUS, Divine Pastor of souls,
You called the Apostles
to make them fishers of people.
Continue to draw to You
ardent and generous souls of Your people
to make them Your followers and ministers;
enable them to share Your thirst for universal
  redemption
through which You daily renew Your sacrifice.

O Lord,
always living to make intercession for us,
open the horizons of the whole world
where the mute supplication of so many hearts
begs for the light of truth and warmth of love.
Responding to Your call,
may they prolong Your mission here below,
build up Your Mystical Body,
which is the Church,
and be the salt of the earth

and the light of the world.
Amen.   Pope Paul VI

Prayer for Religious Vocations**

O **GOD,**
You bestow gifts on human beings
for the upbuilding of Your Church
and the salvation of the whole world.
Pour out Your Spirit
to inspire young people
with the desire to follow You more closely
by embracing the evangelical counsels
of poverty, chastity, and obedience.
Grant Your powerful and continuing assistance
to all who respond to Your call
so that they may remain faithful to their vocation
throughout their lives.
May it lead them to greater fullness
and make them living signs of the new person
in Christ,
freed from money, pleasure, and power,
and outstanding witnesses of Your Kingdom.
Amen.

Mental Prayer

A partial indulgence *is granted to the faithful, who piously spend some time in mental prayer (no. 38).*

Prayer before Mental Prayer**

O **MY God,**
I offer up to You once more
my thoughts, words, and actions

in union with those of Jesus Christ,
that they may be worthy of being received by
   You.
And I renounce every other intention
but such as Jesus would have,
were He upon earth and in my place.

I unite myself,
O my God,
with the Divine Spirit of Jesus,
Who causes You to be loved and adored
by all the Angels and Saints
who fill heaven and earth with Your holy praise.
Through Jesus
may I join with all those creatures that honor You,
and especially with those who honor You
by mental prayer.
Amen.

Prayer for the Pope

℣. Let us pray for our Sovereign Pontiff N.
℟. The Lord preserve him and give him life,
and make him blessed upon the earth,
and deliver him not up to the will of his enemies.

Partial indulgence (no. 39).

O Sacred Banquet

O SACRED banquet,
in which Christ is received,
the memory of of His Passion is renewed,
the mind is filled with grace,
and a pledge of future glory is given to us.

Partial indulgence (no. 40).

Assistance at Sacred Preaching

A partial indulgence *is granted to the faithful, who assist with devotion and attention at the sacred preaching of the Word of God.*

A plenary indulgence *is granted to the faithful, who during the time of a Mission have heard some of the sermons and are present for the solemn close of the Mission (no. 41).*

Prayer before Hearing the Word of God Preached**

O LORD,
grant to Your preacher
a truly mild and judicious eloquence.
Through Your Holy Spirit,
place on his lips
words of consolation, edification, and exhortation.
Enable him to encourage the good to be better,
and to recall to the path of righteousness
those who have strayed.

Enlighten the minds of his listeners
with greater knowledge of You
and fill their hearts
with deeper love for You.
Amen.

First Communion

A plenary indulgence *is granted to the faithful, when they receive Communion for the first time, or when they assist at the sacred ceremonies of a First Communion (no. 42).*

Prayer for First Communicants**

O JESUS,
You loved us so much
that You bequeathed to us the ineffable gift
of the Holy Eucharist.
Look graciously on the young children
who are about to receive You for the first time.

Protect them from the assaults of evil,
strengthen their faith,
increase their love,
and endow them with all the virtues
that will make them worthy to receive You.
Amen.

First Mass of Newly-Ordained Priests

A plenary indulgence *is granted to a priest on the occasion of the first Mass he celebrates with some solemnity and to the faithful who devoutly assist at the same Mass (no. 43).*

Prayer for a Priest at His First Mass**

O HOLY Spirit,
Your servant who is about to celebrate this
Mass
shares the holy priesthood of Jesus
and Your apostolate.
Enkindle in his heart the flames
that transformed the disciples in the Upper
Room.
Let him be no longer an ordinary man
but a man living to transfuse the Divine Life
into the souls of others.

Give him an ardent desire for the inner life
as well as Your consolation and strength.
Enable him to see that even here below
there is no true happiness
unless his life partakes of Yours
and that of the Heart of Jesus
in the bosom of the Father.
Amen.

Prayer for Unity of the Church

ALMIGHTY and merciful God,
You willed that the different nations
should become one people through Your Son.
Grant in Your kindness
that those who glory in being known as Christians
may put aside their differences
and become one in truth and charity,
and that all human beings enlightened by the
true Faith,
may be united in fraternal communion in the
one Church.
Through Christ our Lord.
Amen.

Partial indulgence (no. 44).

Monthly Recollection

*A partial indulgence is granted to the faithful, who
take part in a monthly retreat (no. 45).*

Prayer after a Monthly Day of Recollection**

O JESUS,
I thank You for all the benefits of Your love
that You bestowed upon me this day.
I offer You my whole life
and in particular my labors and sufferings.

Help me to carry out diligently
all the duties of my state
and to direct my entire life
in accord with Your Divine plans for me.

Grant me all the graces I need
to serve You faithfully on earth
and attain everlasting joy with You in heaven.
Amen.

Prayer for the Dead

ETERNAL rest grant to them,
O Lord,
and let perpetual light shine upon them.
May they rest in peace.
Amen.

Partial indulgence, *applicable only to the souls in purgatory (no. 46).*

Prayer for Benefactors

MAY it please You,
O Lord,
to reward with eternal life

all those who do good to us for Your Name's sake.
Amen.

Partial indulgence (no. 47).

Recitation of the Marian Rosary

A plenary indulgence *is granted, if the Rosary is recited in a church or public oratory or in a family group, a religious Community or pious Association;* a partial indulgence *is granted in other circumstances.*

The Rosary is a certain formula of prayer, which is made up of twenty decades of "Hail Marys" with an "Our Father" before each decade, and in which the recitation of each decade is accompanied by pious meditation on a particular Mystery of our Redemption.

The name "Rosary," however, is commonly used in reference to only a quarter part of the twenty decades.

The gaining of the plenary indulgence *is regulated by the following norms: (1) The recitation of a quarter part only of the Rosary suffices; but the five decades must be recited continuously. (2) The vocal recitation must be accompanied by pious meditation on the Mysteries. (3) In public recitation the Mysteries must be announced in the manner customary in the place; for private recitation, however, it suffices if the vocal recitation is accompanied by meditation on the Mysteries (no. 48).*

How To Say the Rosary**

1. Begin on the crucifix and say the Apostles' Creed.
2. On the 1st bead, say 1 Our Father.
3. On the next 3 beads, say Hail Mary.
4. Next say I Glory Be. Then announce and think of the first Mystery and say I our Father.
5. Say 10 Hail Marys and I Glory be to the Father.
6. Announce the second Mystery and continue in the same way until each of the five Mysteries of the selected group or decades is said.

The Five Joyful Mysteries

(Said on Mondays, and Saturdays, and Sundays from Advent until Lent)

The Joyful Mysteries direct our mind to the Son of God, Jesus Christ, our Lord and Savior, Who took human nature from a human mother, Mary. They also bring to our attention some of the extraordinary events that preceded, accompanied, and followed Christ's Birth.

1. The Annunciation

Luke 1: 26-38; Isaiah 7 :10-15

MARY, you received with deep humility
the news of the Angel Gabriel
that you were to be the Mother of God's Son;
obtain for me a similar *humility.*

2. The Visitation

Luke 1:39-56

MARY, you showed true charity in visiting Elizabeth
and remaining with her for three months
before the birth of John the Baptist;
obtain for me the grace to *love my neighbor.*

3. The Birth Jesus

Luke 2:1-14; Matthew 2:1-12; Galatians 4:1-7

JESUS, You lovingly accepted poverty
when You were placed in the manger in the stable
although You were our God and Redeemer;
grant that I may have the *spirit of poverty.*

4. The Presentation in the Temple
Luke 2:22-40

MARY, you obeyed the law of God
in presenting the Child Jesus in the
Temple;
obtain for me the *virtue of obedience.*

5. The Finding in the Temple
Luke 2:42-52

MARY, you were filled with sorrow at the
loss of Jesus
and overwhelmed with joy on finding Him
surrounded by Teachers in the Temple;
obtain for me the *virtue of piety.*

The Five Luminous Mysteries

(Said on Thursdays [except during Lent])

*The Luminous Mysteries recall to our mind important
events of the Public Ministry of Christ through which
He announces the coming of the Kingdom of God, bears
witness to it in His works, and proclaims its demands—
showing that the Mystery of Christ is most evidently a
Mystery of Light.*

1. Christ's Baptism in the Jordan
Matthew 3:13-17; Isaiah 42:1-2, 4-5

JESUS, at Your Baptism in the Jordan,
the Father called You His beloved Son
and the Holy Spirit descended upon You
to invest You with Your mission;
help me to *keep my Baptismal Promises.*

2. Christ's Self-Manifestation at Cana
John 2:1-11

MARY, the first among believers in Christ,
as a result of your intercession at Cana,
your Son changed water into wine
and opened the hearts of the disciples to faith;
obtain for me the grace to *do whatever Jesus says.*

3. Christ's Proclamation of the Kingdom of God
Mark 1:15; Matthew 5:1-11

JESUS, You preached the Kingdom of God
with its call to forgiveness,
inaugurating the ministry of mercy,
which You continue to exercise,
especially through the Sacrament of Reconciliation;
help me to *seek forgiveness for my sins.*

4. The Transfiguration of Our Lord
Matthew 17:1-8; Mark 9:2-8; Luke 9:28-36

JESUS, at Your Transfiguration,
the glory of the Godhead shone forth from
Your face
as the Father commanded the Apostles to hear
You
and be transfigured by the Holy Spirit;
help me to *be a new person in You.*

5. Christ's Institution of the Eucharist
Matthew 26:26-30; 1 Corinthians 11:23-25

JESUS, at the Last Supper, You instituted the
Eucharist,

offering Your Body and Blood as food
under the signs of bread and wine
and testifying to Your love of humanity;
help me to *attain active participation at Mass.*

The Five Sorrowful Mysteries

(Said on Tuesdays and Fridays throughout the year, and daily from Ash Wednesday until Easter Sunday)

The Sorrowful Mysteries recall to our mind the mysterious events surrounding Christ's sacrifice of His life in order that sinful humanity might be reconciled with God.

1. The Agony in the Garden

Matthew 26:36-40

JESUS, in the Garden of Gethsemane,
You suffered a bitter agony because of our sins;
grant me *true contrition.*

2. The Scourging at the Pillar

Matthew 27:24-26; 1 Peter 2:21-25

JESUS, You endured a cruel scourging
and Your flesh was torn by heavy blows;
help me to have the *virtue of purity.*

3. The Crowning with Thorns

Matthew 27:27-31

JESUS, You patiently endured the pain
from the crown of sharp thorns
that was forced upon Your head;
grant me the strength to have *moral courage.*

4. The Carrying of the Cross
Matthew 27:32

JESUS, You willingly carried Your Cross
for love of Your Father and all people;
grant me the *virtue of patience.*

5. The Crucifixion
Matthew 27:33-50; John 19:31-37

JESUS, for love of me
You endured three hours of torture on the Cross
and gave up Your spirit;
grant me the grace of *final perseverance.*

The Five Glorious Mysteries

*(Said on Wednesdays [except during Lent] and the
Sundays from Easter until Advent)*

*The Glorious Mysteries recall to our mind the ratifica-
tion of Christ's sacrifice for the redemption of the world,
and our sharing in the fruits of His sacrifice.*

1. The Resurrection
Mark 16:1-7; John 20:19-31

JESUS, You rose from the dead in triumph
and remained for forty days with Your disciples,
instructing and encouraging them;
increase my *faith.*

2. The Ascension
Mark 16:14-20; Acts 1:1-11

JESUS, in the presence of Mary
and the disciples
You ascended to heaven

to sit at the Father's right hand;
increase the *virtue of hope* in me.

3. The Descent of the Holy Spirit

John 14:23-31; Acts 2:1-11

JESUS, in fulfillment of Your promise
You sent the Holy Spirit upon Mary and the
  disciples
under the form of tongues of fire;
increase my *love for God.*

4. The Assumption

Luke 1:41-50; Psalm 45; Genesis 3:15

MARY, by the power of God
  you were assumed into heaven
and united with your Divine Son;
help me to have *true devotion to you.*

5. The Crowning of the Blessed Virgin

Revelation 12:1; Judith 13:18-20; 15:9-10

MARY, you were crowned Queen of heaven
  by your Divine Son
to the great joy of all the Saints;
obtain *eternal happiness* for me.

*At the end of the Rosary, one may add the prayer
"Hail, Holy Queen," p. 82, and the following prayer:*

Prayer after the Rosary

O GOD,
Whose only-begotten Son,
by His Life, Death, and Resurrection,
has purchased for us the rewards of eternal life;

grant, we beseech You, that,
meditating upon these Mysteries
of the Most Holy Rosary of the Blessed Virgin
   Mary,
we may imitate what they contain
and obtain what they promise,
through the same Christ our Lord.
Amen.

The Litany of the Blessed Virgin, p. 48, may also be said.

Recitation of the Akathist Hymn

In an audience granted to the Cardinal Major Penitentiary on 25 May 1991, the Holy Father Pope John Paul II, by his own supreme authority, approved the decree Paenitentiarae Apostolicae *and ordered that it be published. The decree grants to the Christian faithful who recite the Akathist hymn the indulgence which for the utterly same reason is attached to the recitation of the Marian Rosary, p. 71 (no. 48).*

The following are two of the 24 stanzas that comprise the Hymn.

Mother of the Lamb

HAIL (*or* Rejoice), Mother of the Lamb and the Shepherd.
Hail (*or* Rejoice), sheepfold of the spiritual flocks.
Hail (*or* Rejoice), shelter against invisible enemies.
Hail (*or* Rejoice), entrance to the gates of paradise.
Hail (*or* Rejoice), because heaven embraces earth.
Hail (*or* Rejoice), because earth sings together with heaven.

Hail (*or* Rejoice), perennial voice of the Apostles.

Hail (*or* Rejoice), unshakable courage of the Martyrs.

Hail (*or* Rejoice), solid bulwark of the Faith.

Hail (*or* Rejoice), radiant sign of grace.

Hail (*or* Rejoice), you through whom hell was rendered armorless.

Hail (*or* Rejoice), you through whom we were reinvested with glory.

Hail (*or* Rejoice), O immaculate Bride.

Gate of Heaven

HAIL (*or* Rejoice), pillar of virginity.
Hail (*or* Rejoice), gate of salvation.

Hail (*or* Rejoice), initiator of spiritual fullness.

Hail (*or* Rejoice), dispenser of the Divine goodness.

Hail (*or* Rejoice), because you have regenerated those who were conceived in sin.

Hail (*or* Rejoice), because you have restored wisdom to those who were deprived of reason.

Hail (*or* Rejoice), you who have crushed the corruptor of minds.

Hail (*or* Rejoice), you who have given birth to the source of chastity.

Hail (*or* Rejoice), nuptial bed of pure marriages.

Hail (*or* Rejoice), you who reconcile the faithful to the Lord.

Hail (*or* Rejoice), beautiful nourisher of virgins.

Hail (*or* Rejoice), you who dress the holy souls
as spouses.
Hail (*or* Rejoice), O immaculate Bride.

Jubilees of Priestly Ordination

A plenary indulgence *is granted to a priest, who on
the 25th, 50th and 60th anniversary of his Ordination
renews before God his resolve to fulfill faithfully the
duties of his vocation.*

*If the priest celebrates a jubilee Mass in some solemn
manner, the faithful who assist at it can acquire a* plenary indulgence *(no. 49).*

Prayer on the Anniversary of
Priestly Ordination**

MOST loving Jesus,
today is the anniversary of the day on
which,
despite my unworthiness and through Your
goodness,
You conferred on me the dignity of the priesthood.
You made me not only Your minister
but the voice of Your sublime Wisdom as well,
and the dispenser of Your Mysteries.
My soul is filled with joy, love, and gratitude
for this singular privilege I have received.
At the same time I am sad and troubled
for having so often, and without reason,
failed to respond as I ought
to Your great generosity.

I beg the continual assistance of Your infinite
goodness,

which will enable me to accomplish the sublime
　work
for which You have commissioned me.
With Your light in my mind
and Your strength in my heart
I shall daily dispense in greater abundance
the fruits of Your Redemption to all people.
Amen.

Reading of Sacred Scripture

A partial indulgence is granted to the faithful, who with the veneration due the Divine Word make a spiritual reading from Sacred Scripture. A plenary indulgence is granted, if this reading is continued for at least one half an hour (no. 50).

Prayer before Reading the Scriptures**

COME, Holy Spirit,
　fill the hearts of Your faithful
and enkindle in them the fire of Your love.

℣. Send forth Your Spirit and they shall be
　created.
℟. And You shall renew the face of the earth.

Let us pray.
O God, You instructed the hearts of the faith-
　ful
by the light of the Holy Spirit.
Grant us by the same Spirit
to have a right judgment in all things
and ever to rejoice in His consolation.
Through Christ our Lord.
Amen.

Prayer after Reading the Scriptures**

LET me not,
O Lord,
be puffed up with worldly wisdom,
which passes away.
Grant me the love that never abates,
that I may not choose to know anything
but Jesus, and Him crucified.

I pray You, loving Jesus,
that as You have graciously given me
to drink in with delight the words of Your
   knowledge,
so You would mercifully grant me
to attain one day to You,
the Fountain of all wisdom,
and to appear forever before Your face.
Amen.

Hail, Holy Queen

HAIL, holy Queen, Mother of mercy;
hail, our life, our sweetness, and our hope.
To you do we cry,
poor banished children of Eve.
To you do we send up our sighs,
mourning and weeping in this valley of tears.
Turn then, most gracious Advocate,
your eyes of mercy toward us.
And after this our exile
show unto us the blessed fruit of your womb,
   Jesus.
O clement, O loving, O sweet Virgin Mary.

Partial indulgence (no. 51).

Mary, Help of Those in Need

HOLY Mary,
    help the helpless,
strengthen the fearful,
comfort the sorrowful,
pray for the people,
plead for the clergy,
intercede for all women consecrated to God;
may all who keep your sacred commemoration
experience the might of your assistance.

Partial indulgence (no. 52).

Invocation to Sts. Peter and Paul

HOLY Apostles Peter and Paul,
    intercede for us.

Guard Your people,
who rely on the patronage of Your Apostles
    Peter and Paul,
O Lord,
and keep them under Your continual protec-
    tion.
Through Christ our Lord.
Amen.

Partial indulgence (no. 53).

Veneration of the Saints

*A partial indulgence is granted to the faithful, who
on the feast of any Saint recite in his or her honor the
oration of the Missal or any other approved by legitimate Authority (no. 54).*

Prayer for the Veneration of the Saints**

GOD our Father,
You alone are holy;
without You nothing is good.
Trusting in the prayers of St. N.
we ask You to help us
to become the holy people You call us to be.
Never let us be found undeserving
of the glory You have prepared for us.
Amen.

(Common of Holy Men and Women)

Sign of the Cross

A partial indulgence is granted to the faithful, who devoutly sign themselves with the Sign of the Cross, while saying the customary words (no. 55).

IN the Name of the Father,
and of the Son,
and of the Holy Spirit.
Amen.

We Fly to Your Patronage

WE FLY to your patronage,
O holy Mother of God;
despise not our petitions in our necessities,
but deliver us always from all dangers,
O glorious and blessed Virgin.
Amen.

Partial indulgence (no. 57).

Diocesan Synod

A plenary indulgence *is granted to the faithful, who during the time of the diocesan Synod devoutly visit the church, in which the Synod is being held, and there recite one Our Father and the Creed (no. 58).*

Prayer for Diocesan Synod**

GOD our Father,
You judge Your people with kindness
and rule us with love.
Give a spirit of wisdom
to those You have entrusted with authority
in Your Church
that Your people may come to know the truth
     more fully
and grow in holiness.
Amen.

(Mass for a Council or Synod)

Down in Adoration Falling

A partial indulgence *is granted to the faithful, who devoutly recite the above hymn. But a plenary indulgence is granted on Holy Thursday and on the feast of Corpus Christi, if it is recited in a solemn manner (no. 59).*

DOWN in adoration falling,
     Lo! the sacred Host we hail;
Lo! o'er ancient forms departing,
Newer rites of grace prevail;
Faith for all defects supplying,
Where the feeble senses fail.

To the everlasting Father,
And the Son Who reigns on high,
With the Holy Spirit proceeding
Forth from each eternally,
Be salvation, honor, blessing,
Might and endless majesty. Amen.

℣. You have given them bread from heaven,
℟. Having all sweetness within it.

The minister then says the following (or a similar) Prayer.

Prayer

LORD Jesus Christ,
You gave us the Eucharist
as the memorial of Your Suffering and Death.
May our worship of this Sacrament of Your
Body and Blood
help us to experience the salvation You won for
us
and the peace of the Kingdom
where You live with the Father and the Holy
Spirit,
one God, for ever and ever.
℟. Amen.

(Roman Ritual, *Holy Communion and Worship of
the Eucharist outside Mass*, nos. 97 and 98.)

The Te Deum

YOU are God: we praise You;
You are the Lord: we acclaim You;
You are the eternal Father:
All creation worships You.

To You all Angels, all the Powers of heaven,
Cherubim and Seraphim, sing in endless praise:
Holy, holy, holy, Lord, God of power and might,
heaven and earth are full of Your glory.

The glorious company of Apostles praise You.
The noble fellowship of Prophets praise You.
The white-robed army of Martyrs praise You.

Throughout the world the holy Church acclaims You:
Father, of majesty unbounded,
Your true and only Son, worthy of all worship,
and the Holy Spirit, advocate and guide.

You, Christ, are the King of Glory,
the eternal Son of the Father.
When You became man to set us free
You did not spurn the Virgin's womb.
You overcame the sting of death,
and opened the kingdom of heaven to all believers.
You are seated at God's right hand in glory.
We believe that You will come, and be our judge.

Come then, Lord, and help Your people,
bought with the price of Your own Blood,
and bring us with Your Saints
to glory everlasting.

℣. Save Your people, Lord, and bless Your inheritance.
℟. *Govern and uphold them now and always.*
℣. Day by day we bless You
℟. *We praise Your Name for ever.*

℣. Keep us today, Lord, from all sin.
℟. *Have mercy on us, Lord, have mercy.*
℣. Lord, show us Your love and mercy;
℟. *for we put our trust in You.*
℣. In You, Lord, is our hope:
℟. *and we shall never hope in vain.*

A partial indulgence is granted to the faithful, who recite the Te Deum in thanksgiving. But a plenary indulgence is granted, if the hymn is recited publicly on the last day of the year (no. 60).

Come, Holy Spirit, Creator Blest

COME, Holy Spirit, Creator blest,
And in our souls take up Your rest;
Come with Your grace and heavenly aid
To fill the hearts that You have made.

O Comforter, to You we cry,
O heavenly gift of God Most High,
O fount of life and fire of love,
And sweet anointing from above.

You in Your sevenfold gifts are known;
You, finger of God's hand we own;
You, promise of the Father, You
Who do the tongue with power imbue.

Kindle our senses from above,
And make our hearts o'erflow with love;
With patience firm and virtue high
The weakness of our flesh supply.

Far from us drive the foe we dread,
And grant us Your peace instead;

So shall we not, with You for guide,
Turn from the path of life aside.

Oh, may Your grace on us bestow
The Father and the Son to know;
And You, through endless times confessed,
Of both the eternal Spirit blest.

Now to the Father and the Son,
Who rose from death, be glory given,
With You, O holy Comforter,
Henceforth by all in earth and heaven.
Amen.

A partial indulgence *is granted to the faithful, who devoutly recite the hymn* Come, Holy Spirit, Creator Blest. *But a* plenary indulgence *is granted, if the hymn is recited publicly on the 1st of January and on the feast of Pentecost (no. 61).*

Come, Holy Spirit

C OME, Holy Spirit,
fill the hearts of Your faithful
and kindle in them the fire of Your love.
Amen.

Partial indulgence (no. 62).

Exercise of the Way of the Cross

A plenary indulgence *is granted to the faithful, who make the pious exercise of the Way of the Cross (no. 63).*

Scriptural Way of the Cross**

The Way of the Cross is a devotion in which we meditate on Christ's Passion and Death in order to put their mean-

ing into our lives. This Passion and Death are "revela-tions" of the love of God the Father for all people and of Christ's love for the Father and all people. The devotion of the Way of the Cross should lead us to do in our lives what Jesus did—we must give our lives in the service of others.

Opening Prayer

HEAVENLY Father,
grant that we who meditate on the Passion
    and Death
of Your Son, Jesus Christ,
may imitate in our lives
His love and self-giving to You and to others.
We ask this through Christ our Lord. Amen.

1. Jesus Is Condemned to Death

GOD so loved the world
that He gave His only Son . . .
to save the world through Him.   John 3:16f

He was harshly treated, yet He submitted
and did not open His mouth.
He was silent like a lamb led to the slaughter
or a sheep before the shearers,
and did not open His mouth.   Isaiah 53:7

No one has greater love than this:
to lay down one's life for one's friends.   John 15:13

Let us pray.
Father,
in the flesh of Your Son
You condemned sin.
Grant us the gift of eternal life
in the same Christ our Lord.
Amen.

2. Jesus Bears His Cross

S URELY He took up our infirmities
and carried our sorrows.   Isaiah 53:4

Those who wish to be My followers
must deny their very selves,
take up their cross daily,
and follow Me.   Luke 9:23

Take My yoke upon You,
and learn from Me . . .
for My yoke is easy and My burden is light.
                                        Matthew 11: 28f

Let us pray.
Father,
Your Son Jesus humbled Himself
and became obedient to death.
Teach us to glory above all else in the Cross,
in which is our salvation.
Grant this through Christ our Lord. Amen.

3. Jesus Falls the First Time

H E has broken My teeth with gravel
and trampled Me in the dust.
I have been deprived of peace
and have forgotten what happiness is.
                                    Lamentations 3:16f

The Lord has laid on Him the iniquity of us all.
                                          Isaiah 53:6

Behold, the Lamb of God,
Who takes away the sin of the world.   John 1:29

Let us pray.
Father,
Help us to remain irreproachable in Your sight,

so that we can offer You our body
as a holy and living offering.
We ask this in the Name of Jesus the Lord.
Amen.

4. Jesus Meets His Mother

DID You not know that I must be
in My Father's house?   Luke 2:49

Come, all you who pass by along the road,
look and see
whether there is any pain like My pain.

Lamentations 1:12

You are now in anguish,
but I will see you again.
Then your hearts will rejoice
and no one shall deprive you of your joy.   John 16:22

Let us pray.
Father,
accept the sorrows of the Blessed Virgin Mary,
Mother of Your Son.
May they obtain from Your mercy
every good for our salvation.
Grant this through Christ our Lord. Amen.

5. Jesus Is Helped by Simon

WHATEVER you did for one of the least of
these brothers and sisters of Mine,
you did for Me.   Matthew 25:40

Bear one another's burdens,
and in this way you will fulfill the law of Christ.

Galatians 6:2

A servant is not greater than his master   John 13:16

Let us pray.
Father,
You have first loved us
and You sent Your Son to expiate our sins.
Grant that we may love one another
and bear each other's burdens.
We ask this through Christ our Lord. Amen.

6. Veronica Wipes the Face of Jesus

HIS appearance was disfigured beyond that of any man
and His form marred beyond any human like-
ness.   Isaiah 52:14

Whoever has seen Me has seen the Father.

John 14:9

The Son is the reflection of God's glory,
the exact representation of His being.   Hebrews 1:3

Let us pray.
Heavenly Father,
grant that we may reflect Your Son's glory
and be transformed into His image
so that we may be configured to Him.
We ask this in the Name of Jesus. Amen.

7. Jesus Falls a Second Time

I WAS hard pressed and close to falling,
but the Lord came to My aid.   Psalm 118:13

We do not have a high priest
who is unable to sympathize with our weaknesses,
but One Who has been tested in every way as
    we are,
but without sinning.   Hebrews 4:15

Come to Me,
all you who are weary and overburdened,
and I will give You rest.   Matthew 11:28

Let us pray.
God our Father,
grant that we may walk in the footsteps of Jesus
Who suffered for us
and redeemed us not with gold and silver
but with the price of His own Blood.
We ask this through Christ our Lord. Amen.

8. Jesus Speaks to the Women

DAUGHTERS of Jerusalem,
do not weep for Me,
but for yourselves and your children.   Luke 23:28

Whoever does not abide in Me,
will be thrown away like a withered branch.

                                          John 15:6

You will all come to the same end
[as some Galileans who perished]
unless you repent.   Luke 13:3

Let us pray.
Heavenly Father,
You desire to show mercy rather than anger
toward all who hope in You.
Grant that we may weep for our sins
and merit the grace of Your glory.
We ask this in the Name of Jesus the Lord.
Amen.

9. Jesus Falls a Third Time

MY strength is trickling away like water,
and all My bones are dislocated.
My heart has turned to wax
and melts within Me.
My mouth is as dry as clayware,
and My tongue sticks to My jaws;
You have laid Me down in the dust of death.

Psalm 22:15f

Let your attitude be identical to that of Christ: . . .
He emptied Himself
taking the form of a slave.

Philippians 2:5-7

All who exalt themselves shall be humbled,
and those who humble themselves shall be
exalted.

Luke 14:11

Let us pray.
God our Father,
look with pity on us
who are oppressed by the weight of our sins
and grant us Your forgiveness.
Help us to serve You with our whole heart.
We ask this through Christ our Lord. Amen.

10. Jesus Is Stripped of His Garments

THEY divide My garments among them,
and for My clothing they cast lots.

Psalm 22:19

Those who do not renounce all their possessions
cannot be My disciples.

Psalm 22:19

Put on the Lord Jesus Christ,
and allow no opportunity for the flesh.

Romans 13:14

Let us pray.
Heavenly Father,
let nothing deprive us of Your love—
neither trials nor distress nor persecution.
May we become the wheat of Christ
and be one pure bread.
Grant this through Christ our Lord. Amen.

11. Jesus Is Nailed to the Cross

THEY have pierced My hands and My feet;
I can count all My bones.   Psalm 22:17f

Father, forgive them,
for they do not know what they are doing.   Luke 23:34

I have come down from heaven
not to do My own Will
but to do the Will of Him Who sent Me.

John 6:38

Let us pray.
Heavenly Father,
Your Son reconciled us to You
and to one another.
Help us to embrace His gift of grace
and remain united with You.
We ask this through Christ our Lord. Amen.

12. Jesus Dies on the Cross

WHEN I am lifted up from the earth,
I will draw everyone to Myself.   John 12:32

Father, into Your hands I commend My spirit.
Luke 23:46

He humbled Himself
and became obedient to death,
even death on a cross.
Because of this, God greatly exalted Him.

Philippians 2:8f

Let us pray.
God our Father,
by His Death Your Son has conquered death,
and by His Resurrection He has given us life.
Help us to adore His Death and embrace His
Life.
Grant this in the Name of Jesus the Lord.
Amen.

13. Jesus Is Taken Down from the Cross

THUS it is written that the Messiah would
suffer
and on the third day rise from the dead.   Luke 24:26

Those who love Your law have great peace.

Psalm 119:165

This is how God showed His love:
He sent His only Son to the world . . .
as an atoning sacrifice for our sins.   John 4:9f

Let us pray.
God our Father,
grant that we may be associated in Christ's
Death
so that we may advance toward the Resurrection
with great hope.
We ask this through Christ our Lord. Amen.

14. Jesus Is Placed in the Tomb

UNLESS a grain of wheat falls into the earth
and dies,
it remains just a grain of wheat.
However, if it dies,
it bears much fruit.   John 12:24

When Christ died, He died to sin, once for all.
However, the life He lives, He lives for God.
In the same way, you must regard yourselves
as being dead to sin and alive for God
in Christ Jesus.   Romans 6:10f

Christ . . . was raised to life on the third day
in accordance with the Scriptures.   1 Corinthians 15:4

Let us pray.
Heavenly Father,
You raised Jesus from the dead
through Your Holy Spirit.
Grant life to our mortal bodies
through that same Spirit Who abides in us.
We ask this in the Name of Jesus the Lord.
Amen.

Concluding Prayer

HEAVENLY Father,
You delivered Your Son to the Death of the
Cross
to save us from evil.
Grant us the grace of the Resurrection.
We ask this through Christ our Lord. Amen.

A Night Prayer

VISIT this dwelling,
   we beg You, O Lord,
and drive from it
all snares of the enemy.
Let Your holy Angels dwell herein
to keep us in peace.
And let Your blessing be always upon us.
We ask this through Christ our Lord.
Amen.

Partial indulgence (no. 64).

Visit to the Parochial Church

A plenary indulgence *is granted to the faithful, who devoutly visit the parochial church:*

—on the titular feast;

—on the 2nd of August, when the indulgence of the "Portiuncula" occurs.

Both indulgences can be acquired either on the day designated above or on some other day designated by the Ordinary for the benefit of the faithful.

The same indulgences apply to the Cathedral church and, where there is one, to a Co-Cathedral church, even if they are not parochial churches; they apply to quasi-parochial churches also (no. 65).

Prayer for Visit to a Parochial Church**

GOD our Father,
   in all the churches scattered throughout the
      world
You show forth the One, Holy, Catholic, and
   Apostolic Church.

Through the Gospel and the Eucharist
bring Your people together in the Holy Spirit
and guide us in Your love.

Make us a sign of Your love for all people,
and help us to show forth
the living presence of Christ in the world.
Amen.   *· (Mass for the Local Church)*

Visit to a Church or an Altar on the Day of Its Consecration

A plenary indulgence *is granted to the faithful, who visit a church or an altar on the day itself of its consecration, and there recite one* Our Father *and the* Creed *(no. 66).*

Prayer for a Visit to a Church or an Altar on the Day of Its Consecration**

A LL-POWERFUL, ever-living God,
fill this church with Your love
and give Your help to all who call on You in
    faith.
May the power of Your Word and Sacraments
    in this place
bring strength to the people gathered here.
Amen.   *(Mass for the Dedication of a Church)*

Visit to a Church or Oratory on All Souls Day

A plenary indulgence, *applicable only to the Souls in Purgatory, is granted to the faithful, who on the day dedicated to the Commemoration of all the faithful de-*

parted piously visit a church, a public oratory or—for those entitled to use it—a semipublic oratory (no. 67).

Prayer for a Visit to a Church or Oratory on All Souls Day**

L ORD God,
You are the glory of believers
and the life of the just.
Your Son redeemed us
by dying and rising to life again.
Since our departed brothers and sisters
believed in the mystery of our resurrection,
let them share the joys and blessings
of the life to come.
Amen.   *(Mass of November 2)*

Visit to a Church or Oratory of Religious on the Feast of the Holy Founder

A plenary indulgence *is granted to the faithful, who devoutly visit a church or oratory of Religious on the Feast of the canonized Founder, and there recite one* Our Father *and the* Creed *(no. 69).*

Prayer for a Visit to a Church or Oratory of Religious on the Feast of the Holy Founder**

F ATHER,
each year we recall the dedication of this
church
to Your service.
Let our worship always be sincere
and help us to find Your saving love
in this church.
Amen.   *(Mass for Anniversary of Dedication)*

Renewal of Baptismal Promises

A partial indulgence *is granted to the faithful, who renew their baptismal promises according to any formula in use; but a* plenary indulgence *is granted, if this is done in the celebration of the Paschal Vigil or on the anniversary of one's Baptism (no. 70).*

Text for Renewal of Baptismal Promises*

I, N.N.,
who through the tender mercy of the Eternal Father
was privileged to be baptized
"in the Name of the Lord Jesus"   (Acts 19:5)
and thus to share in the dignity of His Divine
    Sonship,
wish now in the presence of this same loving
    Father
and of His only-begotten Son
to renew in all sincerity the promises I solemnly
    made
at the time of my holy Baptism.

I, therefore, now do once again renounce Satan;
I renounce all his works;
I renounce all his allurements.

I believe in God, the Father almighty,
Creator of heaven and earth.
I believe in Jesus Christ, His only Son, our Lord,
Who was born into this world
and Who suffered and died for my sins
and rose again.

I believe in the Holy Spirit,
the Holy Catholic Church,
the Communion of Saints,
the forgiveness of sins,
the resurrection of the body and life everlasting.

Having been buried with Christ unto death
and raised up with Him unto a new life,
I promise to live no longer for myself
or for that world which is the enemy of God
but for Him Who died for me and rose again,
serving God, my heavenly Father,
faithfully and unto death in the holy Catholic
   Church.

Taught by our Savior's command
and formed by the Word of God,
I now dare to say:

Our Father,
Who art in heaven,
hallowed be Thy Name;
Thy Kingdom come;
Thy Will be done on earth as it is in heaven.
Give us this day our daily bread;
and forgive us our trespasses
as we forgive those who trespass against us;
and lead us not into temptation,
but deliver us from evil.
Amen.

INVOCATIONS—DIRECT LINE TO GOD

Pious invocations are like our own private line to God. We can get in touch with Him at any time and in any circumstance, simply by raising our hearts and minds to Him. The invocation can help us tune into God, but the actual encounter must come from deep within us.

PIOUS INVOCATIONS

*I*N *REGARD to any invocation, the following observations are to be noted:*

(1) An invocation, as far as indulgences are concerned, is no longer considered a work, distinct and complete in itself, but as complementing an action, by which the faithful raise their heart and mind with humble confidence to God in performing their duties or bearing the trials of life. Hence, a pious invocation perfects the inward elevation; both together are as a precious jewel joined to one's ordinary actions to adorn them, or as salt added to them to season them properly.

(2) That invocation is to be preferred which is best suited to the particular situation and one's personal dispositions, whether it is one that comes spontaneously to mind or is chosen from those approved through long-standing use by the faithful and brought together in the following brief list.

(3) An invocation can be of the briefest kind, expressed in one or few words or only thought of mentally.

The following have been taken from pp. 81-84 of the Enchiridion of Indulgences.

Examples of Very Brief Invocations

MY God.

FATHER *(see Romans 8:15 and Galatians 4:6).*

MAY Jesus Christ be praised.

LORD, I believe in You.

I ADORE You.

I PLACE my trust in You.

I LOVE You.

ALL for You.

I THANK You.

THANKS be to God.

MAY God be blessed.

LET us bless the Lord.

YOUR Kingdom come.

YOUR Will be done.

AS THE Lord wills (see Job 1:21).

O GOD, help me.

COMFORT me.

GRACIOUSLY hear me.

HEAR my prayer

SAVE me.

HAVE mercy on me.

O LORD, spare me.

DO NOT permit me to be separated from You.

DO NOT abandon me.

HAIL, Mary.

GLORY to God in the highest.

GREAT are You, O Lord (Judith 16:16; see Psalm 86:10).

Examples of Invocations in Customary Use

WE ADORE You, O Christ,
and we bless You;
because by Your holy Cross
You have redeemed the world.

MAY the Holy Trinity be blessed.

CHRIST conquers!
Christ reigns!
Christ commands!

O HEART of Jesus,
burning with love for us,
inflame our hearts with love for You.

O HEART of Jesus,
I place my trust in You.

HEART of Jesus,
all for You.

MOST Sacred Heart of Jesus,
have mercy on us.

MY GOD
and my all.

O GOD,
have mercy on me, a sinner   (Luke 18:13)

GRANT that I may praise you,
O sacred Virgin;
give me strength against your enemies.

TEACH me to do Your Will,
because You are my God. (Psalm 143:10)

O LORD,
increase our faith. (Luke 17:5)

O LORD,
may we be of one mind in truth
and of one heart in charity.

O LORD,
save us, we are perishing. (Matthew 8:25)

MY LORD
and my God. (John 20:28)

SWEET Heart of Mary,
be my salvation.

GLORY be to the Father,
and to the Son,
and to the Holy Spirit.

JESUS, Mary, Joseph.

JESUS, Mary, Joseph, I give you my heart
and my soul.
Jesus, Mary, Joseph, assist me in my last agony.
Jesus, Mary, Joseph, may I sleep and rest in
peace with you.

JESUS, meek and humble of heart,
make my heart like Your Heart.

MAY the Most Blessed Sacrament
be praised and adored forever.

STAY with us,
O Lord   (Luke 24:29).

MOTHER of Sorrows,
pray for us.

MY Mother,
my Hope.

SEND, O Lord,
laborers into Your harvest   (see Matthew 9:38).

MAY the Virgin Mary together with her
loving Child bless us.

HAIL, O Cross,
our only hope.

ALL You holy men and women of God,
intercede for us.

PRAY for us, O Holy Mother of God,
that we may be made worthy of the
promises of Christ.

FATHER, into Your hands
I commend my spirit.   (Luke 23:46; see Psalm 31:6)

MERCIFUL Lord Jesus,
grant them everlasting rest.

QUEEN conceived without original sin,
pray for us.

HOLY Mother of God, Mary ever Virgin,
intercede for us.

HOLY Mary,
pray for us.

YOU are the Christ,
the Son of the living God.   (Matthew 16:16)

MY JESUS,†
mercy.

VIRGIN Mary, Mother of God,
make us saints.

---

† These last two invocations were added in a footnote in the 1969 English edition.

THE VALUE OF FORMERLY INDULGENCED PRAYERS

All prayers enable us to carry on a dialogue with God. Prayers that were formally indulgenced have an added value because they have been time-tested by the Church and found to be very effective in helping people talk with God or the Saints. They also inculcate spiritual sentiments that work to lessen or do away with temporal punishment due to sin.

FORMERLY INDULGENCED PRAYERS

THIS section (pp. 113-189) contains some of the most ancient and beloved prayers to which indulgences were formerly attached. The Church cut down the vast number of individual prayers because she wished to make the Enchiridion of Indulgences *more manageable.*

At the same time, the Church knew that such prayers fit under the new category of the First General Grant mentioned on p. 13 and are still indulgenced, so to speak.

Those who make use of them with the right attitude continue to gain a partial indulgence. In addition, these prayers are very helpful and filled with sentiments that are fruitful for the faithful.

They possess themes that reinforce the idea of sin and satisfaction for one's sins. They also inculcate the teaching that we are part of the Mystical Body of Christ and the Communion of Saints. In addition, they bring out the fact that the gifts of God are totally gratuitous. Indeed, we can do penance for our sins only through the grace that God gives us.

Finally, these time-tested prayers serve to move us to do good works that are useful not only to ourselves but also to the whole community. In the words of Pope Paul VI:

"An indulgence is not an easy way to avoid the necessary repentance on the part of sinners. Rather it is a help that the faithful who are humbly conscious of their weakness can find in the Mystical Body of Christ, which by charity, example, and prayers works for their conversion" (Letter Sacrosancta Portiunculae, *1966).*

MOST Blessed Trinity,
Father, Son, and Holy Spirit,
kneeling in Your Divine Presence,
we humble ourselves deeply
and beg forgiveness for our sins.

I. We adore You, Almighty *Father,*
and with all our hearts we thank You
for giving us Your Divine Son Jesus
to be our Redeemer.
He gave Himself to us
in the Holy Eucharist
even to the end of the world
and thus revealed to us
the wondrous love of His Heart
in this Mystery of faith and love.
Glory be to the Father, etc.

II. We adore You, *Word of God,*
dear Jesus our Redeemer,
and with all our hearts we thank You
for taking human flesh upon Yourself
and becoming both Priest and Victim
for our redemption,
in the sacrifice of the Cross,
a sacrifice that,

---

† A number within brackets in this section ("Formerly Indulgenced Prayers") indicates the place where the particular prayer may be found in the 1950 edition of the *Enchiridion of Indulgences*

through the great love of Your Sacred Heart,
You renew upon our altars at every moment.
Eternal High Priest, Divine Victim,
give us the grace
to honor Your holy sacrifice
in the most adorable Eucharist
with the devotion of Mary most holy
and Your entire Church,
Triumphant, Suffering, and Militant.
We offer ourselves entirely to You.
Accept our offering
through Your infinite goodness and mercy;
unite it to Your own
and grant us Your blessing.
Glory Be to the Father, etc.

III. We adore You, *Divine Spirit,*
the Paraclete,
and with all our hearts we thank You
for working the unfathomable Mystery
of the Incarnation of the Word of God
with such great love for us,
a blessing that is continually
being extended and increased
in the most Holy Sacrament
of the Eucharist.
By this adorable Mystery of the love
of the Sacred Heart of Jesus,
grant us and all poor sinners
Your holy grace.
Pour forth Your holy gifts upon us
and upon all redeemed souls,
and in a special manner
upon the visible Head of the Church,
the supreme Roman Pontiff,

upon all cardinals, bishops,
and pastors of souls,
upon priests,
and all other servants of the sanctuary.
Amen.
Glory Be to the Father etc.

Consecration   [56]

I VOW and consecrate to God
all that is in me:
my memory and my actions
to God the Father;
my understanding and my words
to God the Son;
my will and my thoughts
to God the Holy Spirit;
my heart, my body, my tongue,
my senses, and all my sorrows
to the sacred Humanity of Jesus Christ,
Who was willing to be betrayed
into the hands of wicked men
and to suffer the torment of the Cross.

St. Francis de Sales

Petition   [69]

ALMIGHTY and Everlasting God,
You have given us, Your servants, grace
by the profession of the true Faith
to acknowledge the glory
of the eternal Trinity,
and in the power of Your Divine Majesty
to worship the Unity.
We beg You to grant that,

by our fidelity in this same Faith,
we may always be defended
from all dangers.
Through Christ our Lord.
Amen.

Morning Prayer [61]

I ADORE You, my God,
and I love You with all my heart.
I give You thanks for creating me,
for making me a Christian,
and for preserving me through the night.
I offer You my actions of this day.
Grant that all of them may be
in accord with Your holy Will
and for Your greater glory.
Save me from sin and from all evil.
Let Your grace be always with me.
Amen.

Night Prayer [63]

I ADORE You, my God,
and I love You with all my heart.
I give You thanks for creating me,
for making me a Christian,
and for preserving me through this day.
Forgive me for the evil I have done today,
and accept whatever good I may have done.
Keep me while I take my rest,
and deliver me from all dangers.
May Your grace be always with me.
Amen.

Union with God   [54]

O LORD our God,
  we offer You our hearts
united in the strongest and sincerest love
of brotherhood.
We pray that Jesus in the Blessed Sacrament
may be established as the center
of our affections,
even as He was for Mary and Joseph.
Finally, O Lord,
may sin never disturb our union on earth;
and may we be eternally united in heaven
with You and Mary and Joseph
and with all Your Saints.
Amen.

Conformed to God's Will   [58]

M OST Holy Trinity, Godhead indivisible,
  Father, Son, and Holy Spirit,
our first beginning and our last end,
You have made us
in Your own image and likeness.
Grant that all the thoughts of our mind,
all the words of our tongues,
all the affections of our hearts,
and all our actions
may be always conformed
to Your most holy Will.
Thus, after seeing You here below
in appearances and in a dark manner
by means of faith,
we may come at last

to contemplate You face to face
in the perfect possession of You
forever in paradise.
Amen.

Invocation to the Divine Persons [53]

OMNIPOTENCE of the Father,
help my weakness and save me
from the depths of misery.
Wisdom of the Son,
direct all my thoughts, words, and deeds.
Love of the Holy Spirit,
be the source of all the activity
of my mind,
that it may be conformed
to God's good pleasure.
Amen.

Acts of Faith, Hope, Love, and Contrition [31]

MY God,
I believe in You,
I hope in You,
and I love You above all things
with all my soul,
with all my heart,
and with all my strength.
I love You because You are infinitely good
and worthy of being loved.
And because I love You,
I repent with all my heart
for having offended You.
Have mercy on me, a sinner.
Amen.

Prayer of Self-Offering to God [52]

TAKE, O Lord,
and receive my entire liberty,
my memory, my understanding, and my whole
will.
All that I am and all that I possess
You have given me.
I surrender it all to You
to be disposed of according to Your Will.
Give me only Your love and Your grace;
with these I will be rich enough
and will desire nothing more.
Amen.   St. Ignatius of Loyola

Prayer for All People [55]

INTO Your hands, O Lord,
and into the hands of Your holy Angels,
I commit and entrust this day my soul,
my relatives and benefactors,
my friends and enemies,
and all Your Catholic people.
O Lord,
through the merits and intercession
of the Blessed Virgin Mary
and of all Your Saints,
keep us from all vicious and unruly desires,
from all sins and temptations of the devil,
and from sudden and unprovided death
and the pains of hell.
Illumine my heart
with the grace of the Holy Spirit.

Grant that I may be ever obedient
to Your Commandments
and never be separated from You, O God,
Who live and reign with God the Father
and the same Holy Spirit forever and ever.
Amen. St. Edmund

Prayer of Adoration to the Trinity [40]

I BELIEVE in You,
I hope in You,
I love You,
I adore You,
O Blessed Trinity, one God.
Have mercy on me now
and at the hour of my death,
and save me.
Amen.

PRAYERS TO GOD THE FATHER

Prayer of Adoration to the Father

O GOD, [46]
I adore You,
and I count myself as nothing
before Your Divine Majesty.
You alone are
Being, Life, Truth, Beauty, and Goodness.

Helpless and unworthy though I am,
I honor, praise, and thank You,
and I love You in union with Your beloved Son,
Jesus Christ, our Savior and our Brother,
in the merciful kindness of His Heart
and through His infinite merits.

I desire
to serve, please, obey, and love You always
in union with Mary Immaculate,
Mother of God and our Mother.
I also desire to love and serve my neighbor
for the love of You.

Give me Your Holy Spirit
to enlighten, correct, and guide me
in the way of Your commandments and holiness,
while I strive for the happiness of heaven
where we shall glorify You forever.
Amen.

Prayer to the Father for Spiritual Growth [66]

HOLY Lord,
Father almighty,
Eternal God,
for the sake of Your generosity
and that of Your Son
Who endured suffering and death for me;
for the sake of the wonderful holiness of His
   Mother
and the merits of all the Saints,
grant to me,
a sinner unworthy of Your blessings,
that I may love You alone
and ever thirst for Your love.
Let me ever have in my heart
the remembrance of the benefits of the Passion.
May I recognize my own sinfulness
and desire to be humbled and deprecated by all.
Let nothing grieve me except sin.
Amen.   St. Bonaventure

Prayer to the Father for the Benefits [68] of Christ's Redemption

ETERNAL Father,
I offer You the infinite satisfaction
that Jesus rendered to Your justice
in behalf of sinners
on the tree of the Cross.
I ask that You would make available
the merits of His Precious Blood

to all guilty souls
to whom sin has brought death.
May they rise again to the life of grace
and glorify You forever.

Eternal Father,
I offer You the fervent devotion
of the Sacred Heart of Jesus
in satisfaction for the lukewarmness and cow-
ardice
of Your chosen people.
By the burning love that made Him suffer death,
may You be pleased to rekindle their hearts,
which are now so lukewarm in Your service,
and to set them on fire with Your love
that they may love You forever.

Eternal Father,
I offer You
the submission of Jesus to Your Will.
Through His merits
may I receive the fullness of all grace
and accomplish Your Will entirely.
Blessed be God!
Amen.   St. Margaret Mary Alacoque

Prayer of St. Thomas Aquinas   [158]
before Communion

A LMIGHTY and ever-living God,
I approach the Sacrament of Your only-
begotten Son,
our Lord Jesus Christ.
I come sick to the doctor of life,

unclean to the fountain of mercy,
blind to the radiance of eternal light,
and poor and needy
to the Lord of heaven and earth.
Lord, in Your great generosity,
heal my sickness, wash away my defilement,
enlighten my blindness, enrich my poverty,
and clothe my nakedness.

May I receive the Bread of Angels,
the King of kings and Lord of lords,
with humble reverence,
with the purity and faith,
the repentance and love,
and the determined purpose
that will help to bring me to salvation.
May I receive the Sacrament
of the Lord's Body and Blood,
and its reality and power.

Kind God,
may I receive the Body of Your only-begotten
    Son,
our Lord Jesus Christ,
born from the womb of the Virgin Mary,
and so be received into His Mystical Body
and numbered among His members.
Loving Father,
as on my earthly pilgrimage
I now receive Your beloved Son
under the veil of a Sacrament,
may I one day see Him face to face in glory,
Who lives and reigns with You forever.
Amen.

Prayer of St. Thomas Aquinas   [160]
after Communion

L ORD,
Father all-powerful and ever-living God,
I thank You,
for even though I am a sinner,
Your unprofitable servant,
not because of my worth
but in the kindness of Your mercy,
You have fed me
with the precious Body and Blood of Your Son,
our Lord Jesus Christ.
I pray that this Holy Communion
may not bring me condemnation and punish-
    ment
but forgiveness and salvation.

May it be a helmet of faith
and a shield of goodwill.
May it purify me from evil ways
and put an end to my evil passions.
May it bring me charity and patience,
humility and obedience,
and growth in the power to do good.
May it be my strong defense
against all my enemies, visible and invisible,
and the perfect calming of all my evil impulses,
bodily and spiritual.
May it unite me more closely to You,
the one true God,
and lead me safely through death
to everlasting happiness with You.

And I pray that You will lead me, a sinner,
to the banquet where You,
with Your Son and Holy Spirit,
are true and perfect light, total fulfillment,
everlasting joy, gladness without end,
and perfect happiness to Your Saints.
Grant this through Christ our Lord. Amen.

Prayer of Petition to the Father [65]

FATHER of mercies,
from Whom comes all that is good,
I offer You my humble prayers
through the most Sacred Heart of Jesus,
Your most beloved Son,
our Lord and Redeemer,
in Whom You are always well pleased
and Who loves You so much.

In Your goodness,
grant me the grace of a lively faith,
a firm hope,
and an ardent love for You
and for my neighbor.
Grant me also the grace
to be truly sorry for all my sins
with a firm purpose of never offending You
    again.
May I thus be able to live always
according to Your Divine good-pleasure,
to do Your most holy Will in all things
with a generous and willing heart,
and to persevere in Your love
to the end of my life. Amen.

Prayer of Union with the Father

O LORD, our God,
we offer You our hearts
united in the strongest and most sincere
fraternal love.
We pray that Jesus in the Blessed Sacrament
may be the daily food of our souls and bodies,
and that He may be established
as the center of our affections,
even as He was for Mary and Joseph.

Finally, O Lord,
may sin never disturb our union on earth;
and may we be united in heaven eternally
with You and Mary and Joseph
and all Your Saints.
Amen.

PRAYERS TO GOD THE SON

Prayer to Center One's Life on Jesus

L ORD Jesus, let me know myself;   [88]
let me know You,
and desire nothing else but You.
Let me hate myself and love You,
and do all things for the sake of You.
Let me humble myself and exalt You,
and think of nothing else but You.
Let me die to myself and live in You,
and take whatever happens as coming from You.
Let me forsake myself and walk after You,
and ever desire to follow You.

Let me flee from myself and turn to You,
that so I may merit to be defended by You.
Let me fear for myself, let me fear You,
and be among those that are chosen by You.
Let me distrust myself and trust in You,
and ever obey for the love of You.
Let me cleave to nothing but You,
and ever be poor because of You.
Look upon me that I may love You,
call me, that I may see You,
and forever possess You, for all eternity.
Amen.   St. Augustine

Conformity to God's Will   [98]

O MOST merciful Jesus,
grant me Your grace.

May it remain with me always
and persevere in me to the end.
Grant that I may always will and desire
whatever is most pleasing and acceptable to
   You.

Let Your Will be mine,
and let my will always follow Yours
and be in perfect conformity with it.
Let my will and desires
always be one with Yours,
and let me be unable to will or not to will
except as You will or do not will.
Amen.   Imitation of Christ, Bk. III, Ch. 15:3

Prayer of Self-Dedication to Jesus Christ [52]

L ORD,
take all my freedom,
my memory, my understanding, and my will.
All that I have and cherish
You have given me.
I surrender it all to be guided by Your Will.

Your grace and Your love
are wealth enough for me.
Give me these, Lord Jesus,
and I ask for nothing more.
Amen.   St. Ignatius Loyola

PRAYERS TO THE SACRED HEART OF JESUS

Prayer of Consecration

I, N . . . , give myself [258]
to the Sacred Heart of our Lord Jesus
Christ,
and I consecrate to Him
my person and my life,
my actions, pains, and sufferings,
so that henceforth I shall be unwilling
to make use of any part of my being
except for the honor, love, and glory
of the Sacred Heart.

My unchanging purpose is to be all His
and to do all things for the love of Him
while renouncing with all my heart
whatever is displeasing to Him.

I take You,
O Sacred Heart,
as the sole object of my love,
the guardian of my life,
the assurance of my salvation,
the remedy of my frailty and inconstancy,
the atonement for all my faults,
and the sure refuge at my death.

O Heart of goodness,
be my justification before God the Father,
and turn away from me
the blows of His righteous anger.

O Heart of love,
I place all my trust in You,
for I fear everything
from my own malice and frailty,
but I hope for all things
from Your mercy and bounty.

Consume in me all that can displease You
or resist Your holy Will.
Let Your pure love imprint You
so profoundly upon my heart
that I shall never be able to forget You
or be separated from You.
May I obtain from all Your loving kindness
the grace of having my name written in You,
for I desire to place in You
all my happiness and all my glory,
living and dying in virtual bondage to You.
Amen.   St. Margaret Mary Alacoque

Joy in the Sacred's Heart's Salvation

[266]

G RANT, we beg You,
Almighty God,
that we who glory in the most Sacred Heart
of Your beloved Son
and call to mind the great benefits
of His love toward us
may find equal joy
in achieving their saving effect.
Through the same Christ our Lord.
Amen.

Prayer for the Blessings of the Sacred Heart

[262]

MOST holy Heart of Jesus,
shower Your blessings abundantly
upon Your Holy Church,
upon the Supreme Pontiff,
and upon all the clergy.
Grant perseverance to the just,
convert sinners,
and enlighten unbelievers.
Bless our relatives, friends, and benefactors.
Assist the dying,
deliver the holy souls in purgatory,
and extend over all hearts
the gentle empire of Your love.
Amen.

Adoration and Petition

[263]

MOST holy Heart of Jesus,
fountain of every blessing,
I adore and love You.
With true sorrow for my sins
I offer You this poor heart of mine.
Make me humble, patient, and pure,
and perfectly obedient to Your Will.

Good Jesus,
grant that I may live in You
and for You.
Protect me amid dangers
and comfort me in my afflictions.
Bestow on me

health of body,
assistance in temporal needs,
Your blessing on all works,
and the grace of a holy death.
Amen.

Commendation of All to the Sacred Heart
[261]

DIVINE Heart of Jesus,
I beg of You to grant
eternal rest to the souls in purgatory,
the final grace to those who are about to die this
    day,
true repentance to sinners,
the light of faith to nonbelievers,
and Your blessing to me
and to all who are dear to me.

To You, therefore,
most merciful Heart of Jesus,
I commend all these souls,
and on their behalf
I offer You all Your merits
together with the merits
of Your most Blessed Mother
and all the Angels and Saints,
together with all the Masses, Communions,
    prayers,
and good works
that are being offered this day
throughout Christendom.
Amen.

M OST merciful Heart of Jesus,
  Divine Seat of Mercy,
for Your sake the Eternal Father has promised
that He would always hear our prayers.
I unite myself to You
in offering to Your Eternal Father
this poor and petty heart of mine,
contrite and humbled in His Divine Presence,
and desirous of making a complete reparation
for the offenses that are committed against
    Him,
especially those that You continually suffer
in the Holy Eucharist,
and most particularly those
that I myself have sadly so often committed.

I wish I could wash them away with my tears,
O Sacred Heart of Jesus,
and blot out with my own heart's blood
the ingratitude with which we all have repaid
Your tender love.
I unite my sorrow, slight as it is,
with the mortal agony
that caused Your sweat to become
as drops of blood in the Garden of Olives
at the thought of our sins.
Offer it, dear Lord,
to Your Eternal Father
in union with Your Sacred Heart.
Render Him infinite thanks
for the manifold blessings
that He constantly bestows upon us,

and let Your love supply
for our lack of thankfulness and remembrance.

Grant me grace always to present myself
in a spirit of deepest reverence
before the face of Your Divine Majesty,
in order to make reparation in some measure
for the irreverences and outrages
that I have dared to commit before You.
Grant also that from this day forward
I may devote myself with all my might
to draw, both by word and by example,
many souls to know You
and to experience the riches of Your Heart.

From this moment
I offer and dedicate myself entirely
to spreading the honor that is due
to Your most sweet Sacred Heart.
I choose It as the object
of all my affections and desires.
From this hour forevermore
I set up my perpetual dwelling in It.
I thank, adore, and love It with all my heart,
for It is the Heart of my Jesus,
Who is worthy of all love,
the Heart of my King and Sovereign Lord,
the Bridegroom of my soul,
my Shepherd and Master,
my truest Friend,
my loving Father,
my sure Guide,
my unfailing Protection,
and my everlasting Blessedness. Amen.

PRAYERS TO JESUS IN THE BLESSED SACRAMENT

Prayer for a Visit to the Blessed Sacrament

L ORD Jesus Christ, [182]
through the love that You bear for us
You remain with us day and night
in this Sacrament,
full of mercy and of love,
expecting, inviting, and receiving
all who come to visit You.
I *believe* that You are present
in the Sacrament of the Altar.
From the depths of my nothingness
I *adore* You,
and I *thank* You for all the favors
that You have bestowed upon me,
particularly for having given me Yourself
in this Sacrament,
for having granted me as my advocate
Your most holy Mother Mary,
and for having called me to visit You
in this church.
I this day *greet* Your most loving Heart
for three reasons:
first, I wish to thank You for this great gift;
second, I wish to make reparation
for all the injuries You have received
from Your enemies in this Sacrament;
and third, I wish by this visit

to adore You in all the places on earth
where You are least honored and most abandoned
in the Holy Sacrament.

My Jesus,
I *love* You with my whole heart.
I am sorry for having so often offended
Your infinite goodness.
I *resolve*, with the help of Your grace,
never to offend You again;
and, at this moment,
miserable as I am,
I *consecrate* my whole being to You.
I give You my entire will,
all my affections and desires,
and all that I have.
From this day onward
do what You want with me
and with whatever belongs to me.
I ask and desire only Your holy love,
the gift of final perseverance,
and the perfect fulfillment of Your Will.
I *recommend* to You the souls in purgatory,
particularly those who were most devoted
to the Blessed Sacrament
and to the Blessed Virgin,
and I also recommend to You
all poor sinners and the dying.
Finally, my dear Savior,
I unite all my affections
with the affections of Your most loving Heart;
and, thus united,
I offer them to Your Eternal Father,

and I entreat Him
in Your Name and for Your sake
to accept them.
Amen.

St. Alphonsus Liguori

Prayer of Adoration and Petition [183]

I ADORE You,
O Jesus,
true God and true Man,
here present in the Holy Eucharist,
as I humbly kneel before You
and unite myself in spirit
with all the faithful on earth
and all the Saints in heaven.
In heartfelt gratitude for so great a blessing,
I love You,
my Jesus,
with my whole soul,
for You are infinitely perfect
and all worthy of my love.

Give me the grace
nevermore in any way to offend You.
Grant that I may be renewed
by Your Eucharistic presence here on earth
and be found worthy to arrive with Mary
at the enjoyment
of Your eternal and blessed presence in heaven.
Amen.

Prayer of Reparation [179]

WITH that deep and humble feeling
which the Faith inspires in me,
O my God and Savior, Jesus Christ,
true God and true Man,
I love You with all my heart,
and I adore You Who are hidden here.

I do so in reparation
for all the irreverences, profanations, and sacrileges
that You receive
in the most august Sacrament of the altar.

I adore You,
O my God,
not so much as You are worthy to be adored,
nor so much as I am bound to do,
but at least as much as I am able.
Would that I could adore You
with the perfect worship
that the Angels in heaven are able to offer You.

O Jesus,
may You be known, adored, loved, and thanked
by all people at every moment
in this Most Holy and Divine Sacrament.
Amen.

PRAYERS TO JESUS CRUCIFIED

Prayer for the Grace of the Passion

O LORD,   [205]
for the redemption of the world,
You willed to be born among human beings,
subjected to the rite of circumcision,
rejected by the people,
betrayed by Judas with a kiss,
bound with cords,
led like an innocent lamb to slaughter,
shamelessly exposed to the gaze of Annas
as well as Caiaphas, Pilate, and Herod,
accused by false witnesses,
tormented by scourges and insults,
spat upon and crowned with thorns,
struck with blows of hand and reed,
blindfolded and stripped of Your garments,
affixed to the wood and lifted high on the Cross,
numbered among thieves,
given gall and vinegar to drink
and pierced by a lance.

Lord,
by these most holy sufferings
that I, Your unworthy servant,
devoutly call to mind,
and by Your holy Cross and Death
deliver us from the pains of hell,
and be pleased to take me
where You took the penitent thief
who was crucified with You.

You live and reign
with the Father and the Holy Spirit,
one God, forever. Amen.

Prayer for Pardon to Jesus Crucified [209]

O MY crucified Lord Jesus,
I kneel at Your feet.
Do not cast me out,
although I come to You as a sinner.
I have offended You much in the past,
but I resolve no longer to do so in the future.

O my God,
I place all my sins before You;
I have considered them and concluded
that they do not deserve pardon.
But I beg You to be mindful of Your sufferings,
which show the value of the Precious Blood
that flows from Your veins.

O my God,
close Your eyes to my lack of merit
and open them to Your infinite merits.
Since You deigned to die for my sins,
graciously grant me forgiveness of all of them,
so that I may no longer feel their burden,
which oppresses me beyond measure.

Help me, my Jesus,
for I desire to become good at any cost.
Uproot, take away, and destroy in me
everything that is contrary to Your Will.
Enlighten me that I may be enabled
to walk in Your holy light all the days of my life.
Amen.

PRAYERS TO GOD THE HOLY SPIRIT

Consecration to the Holy Spirit

HOLY Spirit, [289]
Divine Spirit of light and love,
I consecrate to You
my understanding, heart, and will,
my whole being, for time and for eternity.
May my understanding be always submissive
to Your heavenly inspirations
and to the teaching of the Catholic Church,
of which You are the infallible Guide.

May my heart be ever inflamed
with the love of God
and of my neighbor;
may my will be ever conformed
to the Divine Will;
may my whole life be faithful to the imitation
of the life and virtues
of our Lord and Savior Jesus Christ,
to Whom with the Father and You
be honor and glory forever.
Amen.

Novena to the Holy Spirit [284]

HOLY Spirit,
third Person of the Blessed Trinity,
Spirit of truth, love, and holiness,
proceeding from the Father and the Son,
and equal to Them in all things,

I adore You
and love You with all my heart.

Dearest Holy Spirit,
confiding in Your deep, personal love for me,
I am making this novena
for the following request,
if it should be Your holy Will to grant it:
(mention Your request).

Teach me,
Divine Spirit,
to know and seek my last end;
grant me the holy fear of God
as well as true contrition and patience.
Do not let me fall into sin.
Give me an increase
of faith, hope, and charity,
and bring forth in my soul
all the virtues proper to my state of life.
Make me a faithful disciple of Jesus
and an obedient child of the Church.
Infuse in me efficacious grace
sufficient to keep the Commandments
and to receive the Sacraments worthily.
Bestow upon me the four Cardinal Virtues,
Your Seven Gifts,
Your Twelve Fruits.
Raise me to perfection
in the state of life
to which You have called me,
and lead me through a happy death
to everlasting life.
Through Christ our Lord. Amen.

HOLY Spirit, Divine Consoler,
I adore You as my true God,
just as I adore God the Son.
I bless You by uniting myself
to the blessings that You receive
from the Angels and the Seraphs.
I offer You my whole heart,
and I give You thanks for all the benefits
that You have bestowed
and do unceasingly bestow
upon the world.
You are the Author of all supernatural gifts,
and You enriched
the soul of the Blessed Virgin Mary,
the Mother of God,
with immense favors.

I beg You to visit me
by Your grace and Your love,
and to grant me the Gift of *Wisdom*,
so that I may rightly direct all my actions,
referring them to God as my last end.
Thus, after loving and serving Him as I should
in this life,
I may have the happiness
of possessing Him eternally in the next.

Grant me the Gift of *Understanding*,
so that I may apprehend the Divine Mysteries
and by the contemplation of heavenly things
detach my thoughts and affectations
from the vain things of this world.

Grant me the Gift of *Knowledge,*
so that I may know the things of God
and enlightened by Your holy teachings
may walk without deviation
in the path of eternal salvation.

Grant me the Gift of *Counsel,*
so that I may choose what is most conducive
to my spiritual welfare
and may discover the wiles and snares
of the tempter.

Grant me the Gift of *Fortitude,*
so that I may overcome courageously
all the assaults of the devil
and all the dangers of this world,
which threaten the salvation of my soul.

Grant me the Gift of *Piety,*
so that I may serve You for the future
with increased fervor,
follow Your holy inspirations
with more promptness,
and observe Your Divine Precepts
with greater fidelity.

Grant me the Gift of *Fear of the Lord*,
so that it may act on me as a check
to prevent me from falling back
into my past sins,
for which I ask Your pardon.
Amen.

Archconfraternity of Prayer [282]
to the Holy Spirit

HOLY Spirit, Lord of Light,
from Your clear celestial height,
Your pure beaming radiance give.

Come, O Father of the Poor,
come with the treasures that endure,
come, O Light of all that live.

You of all Consolers best,
and the soul's delightsome Guest,
do refreshing Peace bestow.

You in toil are Comfort sweet,
pleasant coolness in the heat,
Solace in the midst of woe.

Light immortal, Light Divine,
visit now this heart of mine,
and my inmost being fill.

If You take Your grace away,
nothing pure in men will stay,
all their good is turned to ill.

Heal our wounds, our strength renew,
on our dryness pour Your Dew,
wash the stains of guilt away.

Bend the stubborn heart and will,
melt the frozen, warm the chill,
guide the steps that go astray.

On all those who evermore
You confess and You adore,
in Your *Sevenfold Gifts* descend.

Give them Comfort when they die.
Give them Life with You on high,
give them Joys that never end. Amen.

Prayer for the Church [288]

O HOLY Spirit, Creator,
mercifully assist Your Catholic Church,
and by Your supernal power
sustain and confirm her
against the attacks of all her enemies.
By Your love and grace
renew the spirit of Your servants
whom You have anointed,
so that in You
they may glorify the Father
and His only-begotten Son our Lord. Amen.

Prayer to Be Sanctified [290]

C OME, Holy Spirit,
Sanctifier all-powerful and God of love.
You filled the Virgin Mary with grace,
wonderfully transformed the hearts of the
Apostles,
and bestowed miraculous heroism on all the
Martyrs;
come and sanctify us.
Enlighten our minds,
firm up our wills,
cleanse our consciences,
make our judgments right,
set our hearts on fire,
and preserve us from the misfortune
of resisting Your inspirations. Amen.

PRAYERS TO THE BLESSED VIRGIN MARY

Consecration to Mary

MY Queen and Mother,　　　　　　[343]
I give myself entirely to you,
and to show my devotion to you
I consecrate to you
my eyes and ears,
my mouth and my heart
as well as my whole being.

Therefore, loving Mother,
since I am your own,
keep me and guard me
as your property and possession.
Amen.

Three Offerings to Mary　　[336]

HOLIEST Virgin,
with all my heart I praise you
above all the Angels and Saints in paradise
as the Daughter of the Eternal Father,
and I consecrate to you
my soul and all its powers.
Hail Mary . . .

Holiest Virgin,
with all my heart I praise you
above all the Angels and Saints in paradise
as the Mother of the only-begotten Son,

and I consecrate to you *my body with all its senses.*
Hail Mary . . .

Holiest Virgin,
with all my heart I praise you
above all the Angels and Saints in paradise
as the Spouse of the Holy Spirit,
and I consecrate to you
my heart and all its affections,
praying to you to obtain for me
from the Ever Blessed Trinity
all the graces that I need for my salvation.
Hail Mary . . .

Prayer of Dedication to Mary   [343]

MOST holy Mary, my Lady,
I commend my soul and body
to your blessed trust and special custody,
and into the bosom of your mercy,
this day,
every day,
and at the hour of my death.

To you I entrust
all my worries and miseries,
my life and the end of my life.
By your most holy intercession
and by your merits,
may all my actions be directed and disposed
according to your will
and that of your Divine Son.
Amen.

Prayer for a Holy Life [369]

VIRGIN Immaculate,
Mother of God and my Mother,
from your throne in heaven
turn your merciful eyes upon me.
With full confidence in your goodness and power,
I beg you to help me in this journey of life,
which is strewn with dangers for my soul.

I entrust myself completely to you,
that I may never be the devil's slave through sin,
but may always lead a humble and pure life.
I consecrate my heart to you forever,
for my sole desire is
to love your Divine Son Jesus.
O Mary,
since none of your devoted servants has ever
perished,
let me too attain salvation.
Amen.

Prayer to Grow in Grace through Sorrows [385]

MOST holy Virgin and Mother,
your soul was pierced by a sword of sorrow
in the Passion of your Divine Son,
and in His glorious Resurrection
you are filled with never-ending joy
at His triumph.

Obtain for us who call upon you
the grace to partake in the trials of the Church
and the sorrows of the Pope

so that we may be found worthy
to grow in grace
and rejoice with them in the consolations
for which we pray,
in the love and peace of the same Christ our
   Lord.
Amen.

At the Cross Her Station Keeping   [378]

AT the Cross her station keeping,
Stood the mournful Mother weeping,
Close to Jesus to the last.
Through her heart, His sorrow sharing,
All His bitter anguish bearing,
Lo, the piercing sword has passed!

O, how sad and sore distressed,
Was that Mother highly blessed
Of the sole-begotten One.
Christ above in torment hangs,
She beneath beholds the pangs
Of her dying glorious Son.

Is there one who would not weep
'Whelmed in miseries so deep
Christ's dear Mother to behold?
Can the human heart refrain
From partaking in the pain
In that Mother's pain untold?

Bruised, derided, cursed, defiled,
She beheld her tender Child,
All with bloody scourges rent.
For the sins of His own nation

Saw Him hang in desolation
Till His Spirit forth He sent.

O sweet Mother! fount of love,
Touch my spirit from above,
Make my heart with yours accord.
Make me feel as you have felt.
Make my soul to glow and melt
With the love of Christ my Lord.

Holy Mother, pierce me through.
In my heart each wound renew
Of my Savior crucified.
Let me share with you His pain,
Who for all our sins was slain,
Who for me in torments died.

Let me mingle tears with you
Mourning Him Who mourned for me,
All the days that I may live.
By the Cross with you to stay,
There with you to weep and pray,
Is all I ask of you to give.

Virgin of all virgins blest!
Listen to my fond request:
Let me share your grief Divine.
Let me, to my latest breath,
In my body bear the death
Of your dying Son Divine.

Wounded with His every wound,
Steep my soul till it has swooned
In His very Blood away.
Be to me, O Virgin, nigh,

Lest in flames I burn and die,
In His awe-full judgment day.

Christ, when You shall call me hence,
By Your Mother my defense,
Be Your Cross my victory.
While my body here decays,
May my soul Your goodness praise,
Safe in heaven eternally.
Amen. Alleluia.

Prayer for Protection against Evil   [368]

VIRGIN Immaculate,
  you were pleasing in the sight of the Lord
and became His Mother.
Look graciously upon the needy
who implore your mighty patronage.
The wicked serpent,
against whom the first curse was hurled,
continues to wage war and lay snares
for the unhappy children of Eve.

Our Blessed Mother,
our Queen and Advocate,
who from the first instant of your conception
crushed the head of our enemy,
receive the prayers that we all join with yours.
We beg you to offer them at the throne of God,
that we may never fall into the snares
that are laid for us
but may come to the haven of salvation.
In the midst of so many dangers,
may holy Church and Christians everywhere

sing once more the hymn
of deliverance, victory, and peace.
Amen.

Prayer to Our Lady of Reparation [417]

IMMACULATE Virgin, Refuge of sinners,
in order to atone
for the injuries done to Almighty God
and the evils inflicted on human beings by sin,
you accepted with resignation
the death of your Divine Son.
Have pity on us,
and in heaven
(where you reign gloriously)
continue on our behalf
your work of zeal and love.

We want to be your children.
Show yourself a Mother.
Obtain from Jesus, our Divine Redeemer,
that He may be pleased to apply to our souls
the fruits of His Passion and Death,
and deliver us from the bonds of our sins.
May He be
our light in the midst of darkness,
our strength in weakness,
and our refuge in peril.
May He strengthen us by His grace and love
in this world,
and grant us to love Him
in the world to come.
Amen.

Prayer to the Queen of the Holy Rosary [399]

QUEEN of the most holy Rosary,
in these times of such brazen impiety,
show your power
with the signs of your former victories,
and from your throne,
from which you bestow pardon and graces,
mercifully look upon the Church of your Son,
His Vicar on earth,
and every order of clergy and laity,
who are sorely oppressed in this mighty conflict.

Powerful vanquisher of all heresies,
hasten the hour of mercy,
even though the hour of God's justice
is every day provoked
by the countless sins of human beings.

For me who am the least of all,
kneeling before you in prayer,
obtain the grace I need
to live a holy life upon earth
and to reign among the just in heaven.
Meanwhile, together with all faithful Christians
throughout the world,
I greet you and acclaim you
as Queen of the most holy Rosary.

Queen of the most holy Rosary,
pray for us.

Prayer to the Immaculate Heart of Mary [393]

HEART of Mary,
Mother of God and our mother,
Heart most amiable,
delight of the adorable Trinity,
and worthy of all the veneration and tenderness
of Angels and of human beings.
Heart most like the Heart of Jesus,
whose perfect image you are.

Heart full of goodness,
ever compassionate toward our miseries,
deign to warm our cold hearts
and mold them to the likeness of the Heart of
    Jesus.
Infuse into them love of your virtues,
and inflame them with the blessed fire
with which you ever burn.

In you let the holy Church find her safe shelter
and her sweet refuge,
her tower of strength,
impregnable against attacks of her enemies.
Be the road leading to Jesus;
be the channel whereby we receive
all graces needful for our salvation.
Be our helper in need,
our comfort in trouble,
our strength in temptation,
our refuge in persecution,
and our aid in danger.

Especially in the last struggle of our life,
at the moment of our death,

when all hell shall be unchained against us
to snatch away our souls,
in that dread moment,
that hour so terrible,
on which depends our eternity—
then, most tender Virgin,
make us feel
how great is the sweetness of your motherly
    Heart,
how great your power with the Heart of Jesus,
opening to us in the very fount of mercy itself
a safe refuge
so that one day we too may join with you in
    heaven
in praising the Heart of Jesus forever.
Amen.

Prayer to Our Mother of Sorrows   [384]

MARY,
most holy Virgin and Queen of Martyrs,
accept the sincere homage of my childlike love.
Into your heart,
pierced by so many swords,
welcome my poor soul.
Receive it as the companion of your sorrows
at the foot of the Cross,
on which Jesus died
for the redemption of the world.

With you, sorrowful Virgin,
I will gladly suffer

all the trials, sufferings, and afflictions
that it shall please our Lord to send me.
I offer them all to you
in memory of your sorrows
so that every thought of my mind
and every beat of my heart
may be an act of compassion and of love
for you.

Sweet Mother,
have pity on me,
reconcile me to your Divine Son Jesus,
keeping me in His grace,
and assisting me in my last agony,
so that I may meet you in heaven
and sing your glories.
Amen.

PRAYERS TO THE SAINTS

Prayer to
St. Alphonsus Liguori

To Obtain the Fruits of the Redemption

O GLORIOUS St. Alphonsus, [521]
you labored and suffered so much
to assure the fruits of the Redemption
for all human beings.
Look upon the miseries of my poor soul
and have pity on me.
By the powerful intercession that you enjoy
with Jesus and Mary,
help me to obtain true repentance for my sins
together with their pardon and remission,
a profound hatred of sin
and the strength to resist all temptations.

Share with me
at least a spark of that fire of love
wherewith your heart did ever burn;
and grant that, following Your example,
I may make the Will of God
the sole rule of my life.
Obtain for me
a fervent and lasting love of Jesus
and a loving and childlike devotion to Mary,
together with the grace
to pray without ceasing
and to persevere in the service of God
to the very end of my life,

so that I may ultimately be united with you
in praising God and Mary most holy
for all eternity.
Amen.

Prayer to St. Ann [494]

To Perform the Duties of Our State in Life

WITH a heart full of sincere and childlike
love,
I venerate you,
good St. Ann.
You are that beloved and favored creature,
who because of extraordinary virtue and sanctity
received from God the great privilege
of giving life to Mary,
full of grace and blessed among women,
the Mother of the Incarnate Lord.

Because of such great favors,
O most compassionate Saint,
be pleased to receive me
among the number of your devoted servants,
for such I claim to be
and wish to remain for the rest of my life.
Keep me in your loving protection,
and obtain for me from God
the grace to imitate those virtues
with which you were so gloriously adorned.

Help me to know my sins
and to be truly sorry for them.
Obtain for me an ardent love
for Jesus and Mary.

Aid me in observing
the duties of my state in life
faithfully and constantly.
Protect me from all dangers in life
and assist me at the hour of my death,
so that I may safely reach heaven,
where together with you, most blessed mother,
I may praise the Word of God made Man
in the womb of your most pure daughter,
the Blessed Virgin Mary.
Amen.

Prayer to St. Anthony of Padua [532]

To Obtain a Favor

O WONDROUS St. Anthony,
glorious for the fame of your miracles,
you had the happiness of receiving
in your arms
our Blessed Lord
under the guise of a little child.
Obtain for me from God's mercy
this favor that I desire
from the bottom of my heart:
(Mention your request).
Since you were so gracious to poor sinners,
do not regard my lack of merit
but consider the glory of God
that will be exalted once more through you
for the salvation of my soul
and the granting of the petition
that I now earnestly present to you.

As a pledge of my gratitude,
I beg you to accept my promise
to live henceforth more in conformity
with the teachings of the Gospel
and to be devoted to the service of the poor
whom you ever loved
and continue to love so greatly.
Bless this resolution of mine—
and obtain for me the grace
to be faithful to it even until death.
Amen.

Prayer to St. Blase   [537]

To Preserve Our Faith

O GLORIOUS St. Blase,
by your martyrdom
you left to the Church
an illustrious witness to the Faith.
Obtain for us the grace
to preserve this Divine gift within us
and to defend—
without human respect and by both word and
   example—
the truth of that same Faith,
which is so much attacked and slandered
in our day.

You once miraculously healed a little child
who was at the point of death
because of an affliction of the throat.
Grant us your powerful protection
in similar misfortunes.
Above all, obtain for us

the grace of Christian mortification
together with a faithful observance
of the Precepts of the Church,
which may keep us from offending Almighty
God.
Amen.

Prayer to St. Camillus of Lellis [668]

On Behalf of the Sick

O GLORIOUS St. Camillus,
special Patron of the sick poor,
for forty years you dedicated yourself
with truly heroic charity
to relieving their temporal and spiritual needs.
Be pleased to assist them now even more generously,
since You are blessed in heaven
and they have been entrusted by Holy Church
to your powerful protection.

Obtain for them from Almighty God
the healing of all the maladies they suffer,
or at least
the spirit of Christian patience and resignation
that may sanctify and comfort them
in the hour of their passing to eternity.
At the same time,
obtain for us the precious grace
of living and dying
in the practice of Divine love
following your example.
Amen.

Prayer to St. Frances of Rome [570]

To Obtain Detachment from Worldly Vanities

ILLUSTRIOUS St. Frances of Rome,
bright jewel of the Benedictine Order,
you were led by Divine Providence
through various states of life,
that you might be a pattern of every virtue,
to virgins, to matrons, and to widows.

Pray for us to our Divine Savior
that we may be detached from worldly vanities.
Under the guiding hand of our Guardian Angel,
make us grow daily in the love of God,
of His Church, and of our neighbor,
so that one day we may be made partakers
of your happiness in heaven.
Amen.

Prayer to St. Francis of Assisi [517]

To Obtain a Foretaste of Heaven on Earth

O GLORIOUS St. Francis of Assisi,
you generously renounced even in youth
the riches and comforts of home
to follow Jesus more closely
in simplicity and poverty,
in mortification and impassioned love of the
Cross,
and you merited to bear the miraculous Stigmata
in your body.
Obtain for us the grace
to live here below,
as it were insensible to the passing attractions

of all things in this world.
Let our hearts beat with constant love
for Jesus Crucified,
and, in times of gloom and darkness in this life,
lift up our eyes to heaven.
Thus, we may possess even now
a foretaste of the infinite Good
and joys Divine and eternal.
Amen.

Prayer to St. Ignatius Loyola [498]

To Labor for the Greater Glory of God

O GLORIOUS Patriarch, St. Ignatius,
we humbly beseech you
to obtain for us from Almighty God,
above everything else,
deliverance from sin,
which is the greatest of evils,
and secondly, deliverance from the scourges
by which the Lord chastises the sins of His people.

May your example enkindle in our hearts
an effectual desire to employ ourselves continually
in laboring for the greater glory of God
and the good of all human beings.
Obtain for us likewise,
from the loving Heart of Jesus our Lord,
the crown of all other graces,
that is to say,
the grace of final perseverance
and everlasting happiness.
Amen.

Prayer to St. John the Apostle [487]

To Obtain Love for Jesus and Mary

O GLORIOUS Apostle, St. John,
on account of your virginal purity
you were so beloved by Jesus
as to merit to rest your head
upon His Divine breast
and to be left in His stead
as a son to His most Holy Mother.
I beg you to inflame me
with ardent love for Jesus and Mary.

Obtain for me this grace from our Lord,
that with my heart set free from earthly affections
I may even now be made worthy
to be ever united
to Jesus as His faithful disciple
and to Mary as her devoted child
both here on earth and then forever in heaven.
Amen.

Prayer to St. John Baptist de la Salle [540]

To Obtain Fidelity to Christ and the Church

O GLORIOUS St. John Baptist de la Salle,
Apostle of children and young people,
from the heights of heaven
be our guide and our protector.
Intercede for us and help us,
that we may be preserved
from every stain of error and corruption

and remain ever faithful to Jesus Christ
and to the infallible Head of His Church.

Grant that, by practicing the virtues
that you so wondrously exemplified,
we may one day be made partakers
of your glory in heaven, our true home.
Amen.

Prayer to St. Jude the Apostle   [488]

To Obtain the Graces We Need

O GLORIOUS St. Jude,
by those sublime prerogatives
with which you were ennobled in your lifetime,
namely, your kinship
with our Lord Jesus Christ
according to the flesh
and your call to be one of His Apostles,
as well as by the glory
that you now enjoy in heaven
as the reward for your apostolic labors
and your martyrdom,
obtain for us
from the Giver of all good things
the graces of which we stand in need,
and let us store up in our hearts
the Divinely inspired teachings
that you wrote for us in your Epistle.

May we build the edifice of perfection
upon our most holy Faith,
praying by the grace of the Holy Spirit,

and keep ourselves ever in the love of God—
looking for the mercy of Jesus Christ
unto eternal life.

May we strive by every possible means
to help those who have gone astray.
Help us to exalt the glory and majesty,
the dominion and power,
of Him Who is able to keep us without sin
and to present us
without stain and with exceeding joy
at the coming of our Lord Jesus Christ,
the Divine Savior.
Amen.

Prayer to St. Lucy   [562]

*To Safeguard the Light of our Eyes
and our Soul*

DEAR St. Lucy,
your name signifies light,
and this enables us to come to you with confidence.
Obtain for us a holy light
that shall make us careful not to walk
in the ways of sin
nor to remain enshrouded in the darkness of
error.
We ask also,
through your intercession,
for the preservation of the light
of our bodily eyes
and for abundant grace to use our sight

according to God's good pleasure
without any harm to our souls.

Grant, O Lucy,
that, after venerating you
and giving you thanks
for your powerful protection here on earth,
we may come at length to share your joys
in paradise
in the everlasting light of the Lamb of God,
your beloved Bridegroom, Jesus.
Amen.

Prayer to St. Lucy Filippini [578]

To Obtain the Gift of Radiating Christ

DEAR St. Lucy,
you were not content to sanctify yourself
by the fervent and constant practice
of the choicest virtues.
You also zealously dedicated yourself
to the particular mission
of instructing young girls and women
in the Mysteries of the Faith
and the precepts of Christian morality.
Then you founded a special Institute for Teachers,
which was to perpetuate your work
with piety and learning.

Obtain for us
from your Divine Bridegroom
the grace not only to live in a holy manner

but also to pour forth upon other souls
His sweet radiance of light and love,
so that in the evening of our lives
we may close our eyes
to the fleeting light of earth
and open them
to the blessed light of eternity.
Amen.

Prayer to St. Margaret of Cortona [564]

To Obtain Sincere Repentance for Sins

O MOST glorious St. Margaret,
you are the true pearl whom Almighty God
with such great love
snatched from the hand
of the infernal enemy who possessed you
so that by means of your wondrous conversion,
saintly life, and most precious death,
He might inspire all poor sinners to forsake sin
by doing good and avoiding evil
as well as all occasions of sin.

Obtain for us,
your devoted clients,
from your exalted place in heaven,
to which your weeping and your penance lifted
    you,
the grace of a true repentance,
a lively sorrow for our sins,
and after a holy life spent, like yours,
in the love of Jesus Crucified,

the grace of a happy death
and a crown of glory in paradise.
Amen.

Prayer to St. Nicholas of Myra   [551]

To Obtain Help in Our Necessities

GLORIOUS St. Nicholas,
my special protector,
from your throne in glory,
where you enjoy the presence of God,
turn your eyes of mercy upon me
and obtain from our Lord
the graces and helps that I need
in my spiritual and temporal necessities
(and especially this favor . . .
provided it be beneficial for my salvation).

Be mindful, also,
O glorious and saintly Bishop,
of our Sovereign Pontiff,
of Holy Church,
and of all the Christian people.
Bring back to the right path of salvation
all those who are immersed in sin
and blinded by the darkness
of ignorance, error, and heresy.

Console the afflicted,
provide for the needy,
sustain the fearful,
defend the oppressed,
restore health to the sick,
and let all human beings experience

the effects of your powerful intercession
with the supreme Giver
of every good and perfect gift.
Amen.

Prayer to St. Pancratius [555]

To Bring Young People Close to God

O GLORIOUS St. Pancratius,
in the flower of youth,
which for you was especially rich
in the promises of the world,
you magnanimously renounced everything,
to embrace the Faith
and to serve our Lord Jesus Christ
in a spirit of ardent love and profound humility.
Then you joyfully offered your life for Him
in a sublime martyrdom.

Now that you are powerful with God,
hear our prayers.
Obtain for us a living faith
that shall be a steady light upon our earthly
path;
an ardent love of God above all things
and of our neighbor as ourselves;
a spirit of detachment from the good things of
earth
and a contempt for the vanities of this world;
and the grace of true humility
in the exemplary profession of the Christian
life.

We pray to you especially for all young people.
Remember that you are the Patron of youth;
therefore, by your intercession,
make all young people clean of heart
and fervent in piety,
and bring them safe to our Lord.
And for all of us
obtain the happiness of heaven.
Amen.

Prayer to St. Paul of the Cross [510]

To Obtain Devotion to Christ's Passion

O GLORIOUS St. Paul of the Cross,
by meditating on the Passion of Jesus
you reached such a high degree
of holiness on earth
and of happiness in heaven.
And by preaching on the same Passion
you offered anew to the world
the most certain cure for all its ills.

Obtain for us the grace
to keep the Passion ever deeply engraved
in our hearts
so that we may be able to reap the same fruits
both in time and in eternity.
Amen.

Prayer to St. Peregrine Laziosi [553]

To Answer Every Call from God

O GLORIOUS wonderworker,
St. Peregrine,

you answered the Divine call with a ready
    spirit,
forsaking all the comforts of a life of ease
and all the empty honors of the world,
in order to dedicate yourself to God
in the Order of His most holy Mother.
You also labored so diligently
for the salvation of souls
that you merited the title "Apostle of Emilia."
And in union with Jesus Crucified
you endured the most painful sufferings
with such patience
as to deserve to be healed miraculously by Him
with a touch of His Divine hand
from an incurable wound in your leg.

Obtain for us, we pray,
the grace to be ever open to God's inspirations.
Enkindle in our hearts a great zeal
for the salvation of souls.
Deliver us from the infirmities
that so often afflict our poor bodies.
Obtain for us the virtue of resignation
to the sufferings
that it shall please God to send us.
In this way,
imitating your virtues
and tenderly loving our Crucified Lord
and His Sorrowful Mother,
we may be enabled to merit glory everlasting
in paradise.
Amen.

Prayer to St. Tarcisius [557]

To Obtain Love for the Blessed Sacrament

UNVANQUISHED martyr of the Faith,
St. Tarcisius,
you were inflamed with the most intense affection
for the Holy Eucharist
and enjoyed the happiness
of dying united to Jesus in the Eucharistic Species.

We beg you
to obtain for us from our Lord
that our hearts may be filled
with a similar love
in receiving Him frequently into our breast
and above all in the final moments of our lives,
so that united with Him
we may enter into a blessed eternity.
Amen.

Prayer to St. Teresa of Avila [565]

To Obtain Zeal for God's Call

DEAR St. Teresa,
seraphic Virgin,
and beloved spouse of our Crucified Lord,
on earth you were inflamed
with such an intense love
for your God and my God,
and now in paradise
you glow with a brighter and purer flame.

I beg you,
obtain for me also
a spark of that same holy fire,
which shall cause me to forget the world,
all created things,
and even myself,
for you always desired to see Him loved
by all human beings.

Grant that my every thought, desire, and affection
may be continually employed
in doing the Will of God, the supreme Good,
whether I am in joy or in pain,
for He is worthy to be loved and obeyed everlastingly.
Obtain for me this grace,
for you are so powerful with God.
May I be, like you,
all afire with the holy love of God.
Amen.

Prayer to St. Thérèse of Lisieux [576]

To Obtain the Virtue of Purity

WONDERFUL St. Thérèse of the Child Jesus,
in your brief mortal career,
you became a mirror of angelic purity,
of great love,
and of wholehearted surrender to Almighty God.
Now that you are enjoying the reward

of your virtues,
turn a kindly glance upon us who trust in you.

Obtain for us the grace
to keep our hearts and minds pure and clean
like yours
and to abhor in all sincerity
whatever might sully even slightly
the splendor of a virtue so sublime,
a virtue that endears us to your Divine Bridegroom.

Dear Saint,
grant that in every need
we may experience the power of your intercession.
Comfort us in all the bitterness of this life
and especially at its end,
that we may be worthy to share eternal happiness
with you in paradise.
Amen.

Prayer to St. Thomas Aquinas   [520]

To Obtain Understanding of His Teaching

A NGELIC Doctor, St. Thomas,
you are the prince of theologians
and the ideal of philosophers,
the outstanding ornament of the Christian
world
and the light of the Church,
as well as the heavenly Patron

of Catholic schools.
You learned wisdom without guile
and communicated it without envy.
Pray for us to the Son of God,
Who is Wisdom itself,
that, by the coming of the Spirit of Wisdom
    upon us,
we may clearly understand what you have
    taught,
and following your example
put into practice what you have done.

Through the spirit of wisdom,
may we be made partakers
of the teaching and virtue
by which you always shone like a sun on earth.
And let us finally enjoy with you in heaven
the fruits of your merits and labors,
and praise the eternal Wisdom
for all eternity.
Amen.

Prayer to St. Vincent de Paul [513]

To Obtain Help in Affliction

O GLORIOUS St. Vincent,
    heavenly Patron of all charitable associa-
tions
and father of all who are in misery,
while you were on earth you never cast out
any who had recourse to you.
Consider by what evils we are oppressed
and come to our assistance.

Obtain from the Lord
aid for the poor,
help for the sick,
consolation for the afflicted,
protection for the abandoned,
generosity for the rich,
conversion for sinners,
zeal for priests,
peace for the Church,
tranquility for peoples,
and salvation for everyone.

Let all people experience the effects
of your merciful intercession,
so that, being helped by you
in the miseries of this life,
we may be united to you
in the life to come,
where there shall be
no more grief nor weeping nor sorrow,
but only joy and gladness and everlasting happiness.
Amen.

PRAYERS FOR VARIOUS NEEDS

Prayer for Love of God
[106]

MY Lord Jesus Christ,
Son of the living God,
I humbly beg You
to dispel the darkness of my mind
and to give me
lively faith, firm hope, and burning love.

Grant, O my God,
that I may know You well
and do all things in Your light
and according to Your holy Will.
Amen.

For Benefactors
[666]

O LORD,
may it please You
to reward with eternal life
all those who do good to us
for Your Name's sake.
Amen.

Prayer for Choosing a State in Life
[711]

GOD of wisdom and of counsel,
You see in my heart a sincere desire
to please You alone
and to conform myself entirely to Your Will

in the choice of my state in life.
I humbly implore You,
by the intercession of the Blessed Virgin,
my Mother, and my holy Patrons,
grant me the grace
to know what state in life I should choose
and to embrace it when known.

Thus, I may seek Your glory and increase it,
work out my own salvation,
and deserve the heavenly reward
that You have promised
to those who do Your holy Will.
Amen.

Prayer To Obtain the Grace of a Devout Life [716]

GRANT me,
O merciful God,
to desire avidly,
to investigate carefully,
to acknowledge sincerely,
and to fulfill perfectly
those things that are pleasing to You,
for the praise and glory of Your holy Name.

O my God,
order my life;
grant that I may know
what You will have me do,
and help me carry it out,
as is fitting and profitable for my soul.

O Lord, my God,
grant me the grace not to become faint
either in prosperity or in adversity,
so that I may not be made
unduly joyful by the one
nor unduly saddened by the other.
Let me neither rejoice nor grieve
at anything except what leads to You
or leads away from You.
Let me not desire to please anyone
nor fear to displease anyone
except You alone.

Let all things that pass away
seem base in my eyes,
and let all things that are eternal
be dear to me.
Let me turn away from that joy
that is without You,
neither permit me to desire anything
that is outside You.
Let me take delight in the labor
that is for You;
and let me find all repose tiresome
that is without You.

My God,
give me the grace
to direct my heart toward You
and to grieve continually at all my failures,
together with a firm purpose of amendment.

O Lord, my God,
make me obedient without grumbling,
poor without despondency,

chaste without stain,
patient without murmuring,
humble without pretending,
cheerful without dissipation,
serious without undue heaviness,
active without instability,
fearful of You without desperation,
truthful without duplicity,
devoted to good works without presumption,
ready to correct my neighbors
without arrogance,
and to edify them by word and example
without hypocrisy.

Lord God,
give me a watchful heart
that shall not be distracted from You
by vain thoughts;
a generous heart that shall not be drawn down-
  ward
by any unworthy affection;
an upright heart that shall not be led astray
by any perverse intention;
a stout heart that shall not be crushed
by any tribulation,
and a free heart that shall not be claimed
as its own
by any unregulated affection.

O Lord, my God,
bestow upon me
understanding in knowing You,
diligence in seeking You,
wisdom in finding You,

a way of life pleasing to You,
perseverance faithfully waiting for You,
and confidence ready to embrace You
at the last.
Grant that I may be chastised here by penance,
that I may make good use of Your gifts
by Your grace in this life,
and that I may partake of Your joys
in the glory of heaven,
You Who live and reign, one God,
forever and ever.
Amen.   ·   St. Thomas

Prayer for a Christian Family   [707]

GOD of goodness and mercy,
to Your fatherly protection
we commend our family,
our household and all that belongs to us.
We entrust all to Your love and keeping.
Fill our home with Your blessings
as You filled the holy House of Nazareth
with Your presence.

Above all things else,
keep far from us the stain of sin.
We want You alone
to reign over us.
Help each one of us
to obey Your holy laws,
love You sincerely,
and imitate Your example,
the example of Mary,

Your Mother and ours,
and the example of Your holy guardian,
St. Joseph.

Lord,
preserve us and our home
from all evils and misfortunes,
but grant that we may be ever resigned
to Your Divine Will
even in the sorrows
that it may please You to send us,
or in any cross You may permit to come to us.

Finally, give all of us the grace
to live in perfect harmony and charity
toward our neighbor.
Grant that every one of us may
by a holy life
deserve the comfort of Your holy Sacraments
at the hour of death.

Jesus,
bless and protect our family.
Mary,
Mother of grace and mercy,
defend us against the wicked spirit.
Reconcile us with Your Son
and entrust us to His keeping
that we may be made worthy of His promises.
St. Joseph,
foster-father of our Savior,
guardian of His holy Mother,
head of the Holy Family,
intercede for us,

bless us,
and defend our home at all times.
St. Michael,
defend us against all evil
that might threaten our souls.
St. Gabriel,
make us understand the holy Will of God.
St. Raphael,
keep us free from all sickness
and from every danger to our lives.
Our holy Guardian Angels,
keep us safely on the path of salvation
day and night.
Our holy Patrons,
pray for us at the throne of God.

Bless this house,
God the Father,
Who created us,
God the Son,
Who suffered for us upon the Cross,
and God the Holy Spirit,
Who sanctified us in Baptism.
May the one God in three Divine Persons
preserve our bodies,
purify our minds,
direct our hearts,
and bring us all to everlasting life.

Glory be to the Father,
glory be to the Son,
glory be to the Holy Spirit!
Amen.

Prayer to St. Joseph the Worker   [478]
For the Grace To Do our Work Well

GLORIOUS St. Joseph,
model of all those who are devoted to labor,
obtain for me the grace
to work in a spirit of penance
for the expiation of my many sins;
to work conscientiously,
putting the call of duty
above my inclinations;
to work with gratitude and joy,
considering it an honor to employ and develop,
by means of labor,
the gifts received from God;
to work with order,
peace, moderation, and patience,
without ever recoiling
before weariness or difficulties.

Let me work above all
with purity of intention,
and with detachment from self,
having death always before my eyes
and the account that I must render
of time lost,
of talents wasted,
of good omitted,
of vain complacency in success,
so fatal to the work of God.

All for Jesus, all for Mary,
all after Your example, O Patriarch Joseph!
Such shall be my motto in life and in death.
Amen.

Prayer for the Printing of Good Books   [769]

O GLORIOUS Apostle of the Gentiles, St. Paul,

your great zeal at Ephesus led to the burning of books
that you well knew would have corrupted
the minds of the faithful.
Cast a benevolent glance upon us today
and see how an unbelieving and unbridled press
is attempting to take away from our hearts
the precious treasures of the Faith and good morals.

We beg you, O holy Apostle,
enlighten the minds of these misguided writers
so that they may cease doing harm to souls
with their wicked teachings and false insinuations.
Let their hearts abhor the evil they are doing
to the chosen flock of Jesus Christ.

Obtain the grace for us to be ever docile to the voice of the Supreme Pontiff
and never indulge in reading bad books.
Let us seek to read and—insofar as we can—diffuse only good books,
which by their salvific teaching help us to promote
the greater glory of God,
the exaltation of the Church,
and the salvation of souls.
Amen.

INDEX OF PRAYER THEMES

(Bold type indicates the major divisions of this book)